THE CRAFTY GARDENER

THE CRAFTY GARDENER

Inspired Ideas and DIY Crafts from Your Own Backyard

BY BECCA ANDERSON

Mango Publishing
Coral Gables

Published by Mango Publishing Group, a division of Mango Media Inc.

Cover Design: Morgane Leoni
Layout & Design: Morgane Leoni

For permission requests, please contact the publisher at:
Mango Publishing Group
2850 S Douglas Road, 2nd Floor
Coral Gables, FL 33134 USA
info@mango.bz

For special orders, quantity sales, course adoptions and corporate sales, please email the publisher at sales@mango.bz. For trade and wholesale sales, please contact Ingram Publisher Services at customer.service@ingramcontent.com or +1.800.509.4887.

The Crafty Gardener: Inspired Ideas and DIY Crafts from Your Own Backyard

Library of Congress Cataloging-in-Publication number: 2019938541
ISBN: (print) 978-1-63353-870-2, (ebook) 978-1-63353-871-9
BISAC GAR018000, GARDENING / Reference

Printed in the United States of America

This book is not intended as a substitute for the medical advice of physicians. The reader should regularly consult a physician in matters relating to his/her health and particularly with respect to any symptoms that may require diagnosis or medical attention.
(health, alternative healing)

If you want to be happy for an hour,
have a party.
If you want to be happy for a week,
kill your pig and eat it.
But if you want to be happy all your life,
become a gardener.

—Chinese proverb

Contents

INTRODUCTION

Gardening Is the Key to Happiness

**The lesson I have thoroughly learnt,
and wish to pass on to others,
is to know the enduring happiness that
the love of a garden gives.**

—Gertrude Jekyll

Lawns are very high-maintenance and, unless constantly mowed and manicured, can greatly reduce your curb appeal. Besides wasting water and taking up a lot of time, grass in your yard doesn't offer you anything back for all the demands on your time and pocketbook. Lawns also tempt many lawn keepers to use chemicals which are bad for all of us, especially the birds and the bees. Get creative and go at least a little wild. My next-door neighbors overturned and tilled their front lawn and planted potatoes, beets, asparagus, and squash. They love going into the front yard and harvesting fresh veggies for their daily meals. The squash and pumpkins actually have beautiful foliage, and the flowers are stunning and edible as well. Last year, one of their crops grew to "Giant Pumpkin" size and became the talk of the neighborhood as we watched it grow and grow. Needless to say, they had the best jack-o-lantern on the block and some fantastic pies to boot. I am heartened to see the new gardening philosophy of growing veggies, roots stocks, herbs, and berries right beside the roses and lilies. It is gorgeous and supports the bee populations to whom we owe so much.

Gardening, even if it is a hanging basket of cherry tomatoes and a windowsill filled with herb pots, is a much more human way to live, grounded in nature and connected to Mother Earth who provides all. It will definitely add pleasure to your life, and a sense of calm. When I feel stressed, I go out back and do some weeding. It is my therapy, and I can immediately see the profit of my labors. I intend the same for you. With your garden, you are quite literally growing a bounty of blessings.

And so you will find The Crafty Gardener arranged seasonally to help us connect to the rhythms and cycles of natural life. The pleasures of each season are quite different. Spring, the season of new beginnings, is a very active time in the garden for pruning, preparing the soil, and starting seedlings. Summer is the time to really enjoy your garden, to crank up the barbeque, to sit outside on balmy evenings, to invite friends for candlelit dinners on the patio, to enjoy the myriad perfumes your garden gives off; the summer garden is the place to relax and entertain. Fall pleasures are those of a more subtle variety—the harvesting of all your labors, the crisp tang in the air, and the sense of winding down. Winter is fantasy time—the time to hibernate inside, to plan for next year. In each season, garden enjoyments are not restricted to the garden itself. Each season offers a chance to bring the garden indoors. I hope this book inspires you to savor each precious moment and to find new delight in the simple, earthy pleasures that gardening can bring.

CHAPTER ONE

Spring

Spring shows
what God can do
with a drab and dirty world.

—Virgil A. Kraft

IN THE GARDEN

> In the dooryard, an old farm-house
> near the white wash'd palings,
> Stands the lilac-bush tall frowning
> with heart-shaped leaves of rich green
> With many a pointed blossom ringing delicate,
> with the perfume strong I love
> With every leaf a miracle...
>
> —Walt Whitman

Growing Joy: Herbs and Veggies

I have lived in homes where my only gardening options were containers on a deck or planters on the front stoop. This taught me you can do a lot with seed packets, pots, and an open mind. When selecting space for your kitchen garden, you can have something as simple as a set of containers; this can be planned as with any other garden space. If you are lucky enough to have a backyard or land, I suggest you begin the designing process by incorporating all the plants you know you want to use in your magical workings and your cookery, and always allow yourself to experiment. Trying new veggies or seeds can be enormously rewarding. I agree with Londoner Alys Fowler, who is one of England's top gardeners. She says there is no earthly reason why roses and cabbages can't go side by side and veggies can nicely nestle in among florals. Once you have tried a few such painterly plantings, you can give yourself a free hand in your creative approach.

The Art of the Kitchen Garden

What veggies do you love? What are your favorite salad greens? The first rule is to plant what you will actually eat and feel proud to serve to guests. Take your book of shadows and list your preferred herbs, greens, vegetables (including root vegetables), fruits, and herbs. Now, strike out anything you can buy really cheaply—no sense in using valuable space for something easily available at a lower price than the cost of growing it. Another caution: check out your soil type. Carrots need deep, rich soil to grow well. If your lot has shallow and sandy soil, cross carrots off your list and look to surface crops like potatoes and beets instead.

Here are the vegetables anyone can grow, from beginners to pros with their own greenhouses:

Lettuce, peas, onions, beets, potatoes, beans, and radishes.

Lettuce leaves for your salads are the easiest edible crop to grow. A few varieties will be ready to harvest in weeks! Choose a seed mix that will give you a variety of leaves for different tastes, colors, and textures. For best results, sow in stages so you don't get loads all at once. Sow a couple of lanes every few weeks throughout the summer to ensure a continuous supply.

Once you are a pro with lettuce, grow spinach and rocket for your salad bowl.

Peas are a trouble-free crop that can handle cooler weather, so you can skip the step of starting the seedlings indoors. Simply sow the seeds in the ground from March onward and watch them thrive. The plants will need support—put in stakes or chicken wire attached to posts, and occasionally wind the stems around as they grow. Harvest your fresh peas from June to August—the more you pick, the more will grow.

Onions are problem-free and easy to propagate. After your seedlings sprout, thin seedlings to an inch apart, and thin again in four weeks to six inches apart. Onions are a staple for cooking, so you and your family will be grateful once you have established an onion patch in your kitchen garden.

Potatoes and beets give a high return for your labor. To me, the best way to grow both is the world's laziest way to garden; I remember reading about it when I was ten, in a book by

Thalassa Crusoe, a pioneering organic gardener. I was fascinated that you could grow root vegetables without even needing to turn any soil. You can grow potatoes, yams, etc. under straw! Simply cut up mature potatoes that have "eyes" or the fleshy tubers sprouting out of the flesh of the potato, making sure each piece has an eye. After you "plant" or place the seed potato chunks on the ground, put loose straw over the pieces and between all the rows, at least four to six inches deep. When the seed pieces start growing, your potato sprouts will emerge through the straw cover. How easy was that? Crusoe also said you could do the same under wet, shredded newspaper, but straw is more organic.

Radishes have enjoyed a new popularity thanks to Korean and Japanese cuisine. They add a fun pop of spicy, tangy flavor to soups, stews, tempura, and salads, and are also tasty all on their own. They can grow equally well in the ground in spring or in a pot. Radishes like a lot of sun and well-drained soil. They are also a crop you can grow in several waves per season. If you keep the soil moist, you'll have big beautiful radishes to brighten any dish.

Green beans are the opposite of the low-maintenance beets and potatoes, as they will need staking or poles for support. However, an easier path to a great crop of green beans can be to grow them in a five-gallon container. After they have reached four or five feet long, place a pole or stake carefully in the pot and allow the bean vines to wind around it. Soon you'll have a pot of beans even Grandma might recognize as a favorite vegetable for any occasion.

HARBINGERS OF SPRING

One of my favorite times in my flower garden is pre-bloom time. The blush on the plant about to bloom starts to glow. It resembles a young girl of that certain age—twelve? thirteen?—just starting to fill out, grow up, straining to show her hidden promise. Then, a shine and dominance as it pushes everything out of the way to say, "Watch out world, here I come!" Tomorrow or the next day, I know it will be soon. Its arms reach out to the warm sun and soft spring rains. Everything surrounding it stays down and low, letting this one have its turn in the sun. I wait anxiously for the peak to arrive. Tomorrow?

> One of the most delightful things about a garden is the anticipation it provides.
>
> —W. E. Johns

SIGNS OF THE NEW SEASON

Nature signals the return of spring to each of us in a different way. For some, it is the blooming of a redbud or forsythia; for others, it is the determined daffodil, who is the trumpeter of spring, in bold pre-Easter yellow. For me, it is the dogwood tree, budding up everywhere with pink-infused blossoms of thickest cream. I love that the dogwood is such a democrat, growing anywhere and everywhere, in places where no other such beauty dare show herself.

> A man ought to carry himself in the world as an orange tree would if it could walk up and down in the garden, swinging perfume from every little censer it holds up in the air.
>
> **—Henry Ward Beecher**

HOW TO GROW A WILDFLOWER MEADOW

I believe having a lawn is vastly overrated. It takes a tremendous amount of water and too much labor and causes vast quantities of chemicals to be dumped into our water supply. So I decided to dig mine up and plant a wildflower meadow instead. It took some work to get it going, but within four weeks, I had my first bloom. It was a glorious sight for six months and, unlike a lawn, is virtually maintenance-free. Plus I had an almost endless supply of cut flowers from late spring to late fall.

The tricks are to till the soil in the spring, select a pure wildflower mix (no grass or vermiculite filler) appropriate to your growing area, and blend the seed with four times its volume of fine sand, so it will disperse evenly. After you've spread it over the dirt, put down a layer of loose hay to keep the seeds from blowing away. Usually the mixes are a combination of annuals, biannuals, and perennials. To keep the annuals going, you have to rough up parts of the soil and reseed just those every year.

> To be overcome by the fragrance of flowers is a delectable form of defeat.
>
> **—Beverley Nichols**

SUN-INFUSED FLOWER ESSENCES

For centuries, flower essences have been used to heal many infirmities (see list below). While the health-food-store versions are handy, they are also very spendy. You can make your own flower essences at home. Start by making a mother tincture—the most concentrated form of the essence—which can then be used to make stock bottles. The stock bottles are used to make dosage bottles for the most diluted form of the essence, which is the one you actually take.

What you will need to make a sun-infused essence:

- Fresh pure water or distilled water, 3 quarts
- Clear glass 2 ½-quart mixing bowl
- A dark green, blue, or green glass 8-ounce sealable bottle
- Organic brandy or vodka
- Freshly picked flowers specific to the malady being treated
- Clean, dry cheesecloth for straining

Ideally, you begin early in the morning, with your chosen flowers picked by nine o'clock at the latest. This ensures three hours of sunlight before the noon hour, after which the sunlight is less effective and can even drain the energy.

Fill the bowl with the fresh water. To avoid touching them, gingerly place the flowers on the surface of the water, using tweezers or chopsticks very carefully, and add until the surface is covered. Let the bowl sit in the sun for three to four hours or until the flowers begin to fade.

Now, delicately remove the flowers, being careful not to touch the water. Half-fill your colored-glass bottle with the strained flower essence water and top the other half off with the organic brandy or vodka (40 percent/80 proof is advised to prolong the shelf life to three months if stored in a cool, dark cupboard). This is your mother tincture; label it with the date and the name of the flower, such as "Rose Water, July 14, 2018." Use any remaining essence water, and murmur a prayer of gratitude for their beauty and healing power.

To make a stock bottle from your mother tincture, fill a 30-ml dropper bottle ¾ with brandy and ¼ with spring water, then add three drops of the mother tincture. This will last at least three months and enable you to make lots of dosage bottles, which contain the solutions you actually take.

To make the dosage bottle for any flower essence, just add two or three drops from the stock bottle to another 30-ml dropper bottle of ¼ brandy and ¾ distilled water. Any time you need some of this gentle medicine, place four drops of this solution under your tongue or sip it in a glass of water four times a day or as often as you feel the need. You can't overdose on flower remedies, though more frequent, rather than larger, doses are much more effective.

Flower essences mixed with 30 milliliters distilled water can also be used as the following remedies:

- Addiction: *skullcap, agrimony*
- Anger: *nettle, blue flag, chamomile*
- Anxiety: *garlic, rosemary, aspen, periwinkle, lemon balm, white chestnut, gentian*
- Bereavement: *honeysuckle*
- Depression: *borage, sunflower, larch, chamomile, geranium, yerba santa, black cohosh, lavender, mustard*
- Exhaustion: *aloe, yarrow, olive, sweet chestnut*
- Fear: *poppy, mallow, ginger, peony, water lily, basil, datura*
- Heartbreak: *heartsease, hawthorn, borage*
- Lethargy: *aloe, thyme, peppermint*
- Stress: *dill, echinacea, thyme, mistletoe, lemon balm*
- Spiritual blocks: *oak, ginseng, lady's slipper*

THE GARDEN OF EARTHLY DELIGHTS

I have always been extremely sensitive to smells. Blessed (or cursed) by a finely tuned sense of smell, I find I am often led around by my nose. I have fallen in love because of the way a man smelled; when I was a child and my parents were away on a trip, I used to steal into their bedroom and smell their robes hanging on the back of the door. One of my favorite books is *Perfume*, the story of a man so affected by scents he can smell them from hundreds of miles away.

Naturally enough, I am attracted to flowers primarily for their scent. All my roses are chosen for odor—spicy sweet, musky, peppery—if they don't smell good, I don't want them. My current favorite is a climber called Angel Face. I also love the heady smell of lavender, the spiciness of daffodils, the romance of lilacs and lilies of the valley, and the subtlety of certain bearded irises. I particularly love the elusiveness of fragrance. You catch a scent in the garden and follow your nose to…where? Now it's here; then it's gone. That's why I love the sweet olive tree that blooms in Southern California in the early spring. The fragrance is strong in the early evening as you walk down the street, but press your nose against a blossom and the scent diminishes.

My husband, who knows of my fragrance passion, surprised me last spring by planting me a huge patch of multicolored sweet peas and an entire bed of rubrum and Casablanca lilies. Batches of sweet peas perfumed my office throughout the spring. Extremely long-lasting as cut flowers, the lilies bloomed for two solid months during the summer and, all that time, the house was full of their heady scent. I don't think any gift has ever pleased me more.

> And because the breath of flowers is far sweeter In the air (where it comes and goes, like the warbling of music) than in the hand, therefore, nothing is more fit for that delight than to know what be the flowers and plants that do best perfume the air.
>
> —Francis Bacon

FRAGRANT PLANTS

Smell is so individual—I love narcissus, but know many people who can't stand it, and folks wax eloquent about wisteria, the smell of which makes me sick. So, in creating a fragrant garden, let your nose be your guide. Here are some suggestions: jasmine, honeysuckle, sweet autumn clematis, mimosa, hosta, stock, evening primrose, nicotiana, angel's trumpet (especially the white), moonflower, sweet pea, ginger, lily of the valley, peony, and pinks.

DIY INSPIRED IDEA: THE SCENT OF HAPPINESS

The minute you walk into someone's home, you can almost immediately tell how happy a household it is. Much of that is determined by the smell. A home with the fragrance of sugar cookies or a freshly baked pumpkin pie is one you may well want to visit often. Similarly, a space redolent of the bouquet of lilies or tea roses is one where the residents take care to make their home beautiful to both the eye and the other senses. There are lots of small things we can do in regard to "energy maintenance" for our home. To sweeten any mood, this recipe works wonders on you or anyone in your environment who might need a lift. Combine the following essential oils in a quart spray bottle filled with water:

- **Two drops Neroli**
- **Four drops bergamot**
- **Four drops lavender**
- **Two drops rosemary**

> Working in the garden gives me something beyond the enjoyment of senses. It gives me a profound feeling of inner peace.
>
> **—Ruth Stout**

PAINTERLY PRIMROSES

As a young girl, I was particularly taken by a row of primroses my mother had in a border planting. The colors were deep and pure like my favorite crayons—purplish blues, intense red-orange, and buttery yellows. I loved that such beauty came up out of rather commonplace and cabbagey foliage. When Mom showed me how to carefully separate the "babies" from the established adult primroses, I planted my very own, in my favorite mysterious blue, in "my" part of the garden. Mom, who ran a small but busy dairy farm, also showed me her secrets of accelerating plant growth without the blue hormone-filled potions you could buy at the hardware store. (That was cheating in her book.) She would take well-"cured" cow dung and mix it into the soil around her plants. I took her cue, and by the next spring, I had a prim little row of primroses that had all sprung from the baby I had brought home and transplanted. It was at that point that my mom nodded approvingly and I was pronounced to have a green thumb.

> One of the daintiest joys of spring is the falling of soft rain among blossoms.
>
> **—Mary Webb**

A BED FOR YOUR FLOWERS

I found an old bed in a neighbor's trash. It was wrought ironwork that was very intricate and just too pretty to be thrown away. I set the footboard and headboard at each end of a row of flowers in one of my gardens. When a passerby asks me why the bed is in the middle of my garden, I reply with, "Haven't you ever heard of a flower bed?" I now have an herb bed, too. I'm looking for an old crib to set around my seedlings, and that will be my nursery bed.

> The first gathering of salads, radishes, and herbs make me feel like a mother about her baby—how could anything so beautiful be mine?
>
> **—Alice B. Toklas**

TRUMPETING JOY WITH TULIPS

I love tulips better than any other spring flower. They are the embodiment of alert cheerfulness and tidy grace, and next to a hyacinth they look like wholesome, freshly scrubbed young girls beside stout ladies whose every movement weighs down the air with patchouli. Their faint, delicate scent is refinement itself; and is there anything in the world more charming than the sprightly way they hold up their little faces to the sun? I have heard them called bold and flaunting. But to me they seem modest grace itself, only always on the alert to enjoy life as much as they can and unafraid of looking the sun or anything else above them in the face.

> To dig one's own spade into one's own earth! Has life anything better to offer than this?
>
> **—Beverly Nichols**

SOUND GARDENING

If you want a more sophisticated sound for your garden than wind chimes normally offer, consider garden bells. They are a set of cup-shaped metal bells on wires that comes with a base. Like chimes, they peal when blown by the breeze. Unlike chimes, however, the tones change when they are filled with rain, and their sound can be adjusted by bending the wires.

WIND CHIME FENG SHUI: INVITING GOOD ENERGY INTO YOUR HOME

Make a wind chime of "shiny objects" such as old keys, bits of jewelry, and other items from your decluttering. For example, I have a lot of "mateless" earrings which I love even though they are only one of a pair. These chimes abet gathering up the good energy of those unseen that can help protect you and drive away the not-so-helpful energy. Take a stick (a small piece of sea-smoothed driftwood is perfect); tie string around the shiny objects and hang them from the stick where they can tinkle gently in the breeze and make contact with your garden's guardian angels for you. Hang it in a window in your home or wherever you want to hear the lovely music of your wind chimes.

> And all it lends to the sky is this—
> A sunbeam giving the air a kiss.
>
> **—Harry Kemp, "The Hummingbird"**

A SPRING REVERIE

In the enclosure, the spring flowers are almost too beautiful—a great stretch of foam-like cowslips. As I bend over them, the air is heavy and sweet with their scent, like hay and new milk and the kisses of children, and, further on, a sunlit wonder of chiming daffodils.

Before me are two great rhododendron bushes. Against the dark, broad leaves the blossoms rise, flame-like, tremulous in the still air, and the pear rose loving-cup of a magnolia hands delicately on the gray bough.

> May all your weeds be wildflowers.
>
> **—Gardening plaque**

PUT A WREATH ON IT

Oftentimes, your kitchen is the heart of the home. Something about cooking and sharing food brings people together. An herbal wreath hanging on the kitchen door can be a source of love and luck. You'll need the following for your creation:

- **Freshly cut herbs of your choice**
- **A wire wreath frame, available from most craft stores**
- **Either string or florist's wire, ribbon, and a hot glue gun**

This is truly one of the simplest craft projects you can ever make—simply use the wreath frame as a base and use string or the florist's wire to anchor the fresh herbs into place. Finish it off with a colorful ribbon, or other magical decorative touches you may want to add.

Healing Wreath: The ideal herbs for a wreath that brings curative properties include lavender, barley, comfrey, rosemary, peppermint, borage, olive, eucalyptus, and apple blossom. Brown and green ribbon adds a touch of healing color.

Protection Wreath: Hang this guardian wreath on your front door using heather, holly, dill, foxglove, garlic, sandalwood, snapdragon, mustard, foxglove, mistletoe, and/or mugwort. White and blue ribbons add security and serenity.

Abundance Wreath: Greet prosperity at the door with herbs associated with money magic, which include clover, chamomile, sunflower, apple, cinnamon, myrtle, basil, and bay leaf. Weave in gold and green ribbon to add to your luck.

Love Wreath: Don't wait until Valentine's Day to try this; love should be 24/7, 365. Invite love into your home by hanging a wreath full of love herbs on your door. Any combination of these will work beautifully. I recommend using herbs that personally resonate for you among these options: allspice, clove, catnip, fig, bleeding heart, periwinkle, tulip, peppermint, violet, daffodil, lavender, and marjoram. Adorn with pink and red ribbons to let the universe know you're ready to welcome love into your life.

FOR LOVE OF WEEDS

As I work in my vegetable garden, tenderly planting seedlings of peppers, cucumbers, and tomatoes, I suddenly spot the weeds and regretfully rip them out by their roots. Regretfully because I'm a great fan of weeds. Weeds are the wonder workers of the world. Weeds covered the hellhole of Hiroshima with a living green carpet of hope. Within a year after the volcanic explosion, weeds brightened the miles of volcanic ash around Mount St. Helen's. As I stood in Yellowstone, disconsolately peering at a desolate forest of giants blackened by the great fire, my eye fastened on small clumps of green—patches of weeds whispering on the winds, "We will be back."

> Rain in spring is as precious as oil.
>
> —Chinese proverb

SURPRISE GUESTS

I strive to be an urban gardener, but rarely do much better than a pot of basil and a few annuals in my window boxes. However, I discovered a toil-free pleasure in my back patio. Since we live in an older building, there are a bunch of old planters filled with dirt and scruffy remains of plants. One day, I decided to water these planters and was pleasantly rewarded a week or so later with a profusion of mostly weeds but some flowers. One box even yielded a red tulip this spring. Even the weeds are pretty, and one bunch has tiny orange flowers on spindly branches. All it took was a little time and a little water. I enjoy the daily anticipation as new things reveal themselves, and, besides, it's far prettier than the brown scruffy stuff.

> To win the secret of a weed's plain heart.
>
> —James Russell Lowell

BOTTLE YOUR OWN BASIL INFUSION OIL

Infusion is a trendy cooking method that brings the flavors of one food, in this case, fresh herbs, to another, such as oil. Basil oil is unbelievably easy to make. You'll need:

- **¾ cup virgin olive oil (you can use safflower oil or canola)**
- **2 ounces fresh basil**

Ideally, you gather your fresh herbs in your own kitchen garden, but any farmers' market or organic grocery will have green herbs. For the best and purest flavor, use fresh herbs at their peak. Rinse thoroughly in cold water. Gently pat dry with paper towels and give the basil a coarse chopping. Place into a metal colander and dip into boiling water for 10 seconds. Rinse in an ice-water bath and drain well. Gently pat the basil dry and add it to the oil. After three to five days in a cool, dark place, the flavor will have infused into the oil, adding the fresh, bright green note of the herbs. Use liberally on roasts and salads, and drizzle on top of cooked vegetables and soups. Basil not only confers much palatability, but it also brings prosperity. Enjoy!

These herbs also make fantastic infused oils: rosemary. tarragon, parsley, chives, and cilantro.

URBAN GARDENING: PRODUCE FOR APARTMENT DWELLERS

If you have no space or time for a garden (or are plagued by critters eating your goodies before you get to them), try creating hanging vegetable baskets. According to experts, almost anything can be grown in a basket, but be sure to get compact-growing varieties of the vegetables you want. Buy fourteen-inch-diameter wire baskets (sixteen-inch for zucchini or watermelons). It's best to grow one type of vegetable per basket, although a variety of lettuces or herbs will work well together.

Line baskets with sphagnum moss and fill with potting soil. Plant seedlings rather than seeds, and hang the baskets outdoors from patios or rafters where they will get at least four hours of afternoon sun. Avoid overwatering seedlings, but once they become established, be aware that you need to feed and water frequently; on the hottest days, they may even need to be watered twice a day! Once seedlings are three weeks old, fertilize every three weeks with an all-purpose soluble fertilizer, but never feed unless the soil is damp.

> To be beautiful and to be calm, without mental fear, is the ideal of nature.
>
> —Richard Jefferies

EASY-CARE GARDENING

Too busy to care for a vegetable garden on your own or don't have the room? Consider what one hundred thousand folks around the United States do—"buy" shares in someone's large garden. All shareholders agree to pay a certain amount per year and in exchange get weekly baskets of produce. Depending on where you live, deliveries can be anywhere from twenty-two to fifty-two weeks per year.

Like most good ideas, this one has a name—Community-Supported Agriculture—and an organization, CSANA. According to CSANA, shares usually cost between three and six hundred dollars per year. (Many offer discounts for labor, since the work is shared, no one is overburdened, and there's the added bonus of meeting fellow gardeners you might not otherwise know.) For more information about the six hundred farms that belong to CSANA, contact them at (413) 538-4374 or email to csnana@bcn.net. Their web address is http://www.umass.edu/umext/CSA.

> I am not...certain that I want to be able to identify
> all of the warblers. There is a charm sometimes
> in not knowing who the singer is.
>
> **—Donald Culross Peattie**

REMEMBERING LILACS

I suppose the garden behind my grandparents' house was small, but to a four-year-old it seemed immense. The distance from the back door to the end of the yard was a journey from the safety of home, across an expanse of grass, around orderly flower beds, and finally to the marvelous wilderness of the tall, old lilac hedge. I discovered that a persistent push would let me enter a cool, green space under the branches of the lilacs. There I daily established my first household, presiding over tea parties for an odd assortment of stuffed animals and the patient family cat.

Now, nearly seven decades later, the heady scent of lilacs takes me back to that garden where I took those first ventures toward independence—though never out of sight of the familiar back door.

> Unless the soul goes out to meet what we see
> we do not see it; nothing do we see, not a beetle, not
> a blade of grass.
>
> **—William Henry Hudson**

HOUSE BLESSING: FARMERS' MARKET POTPOURRI

Even if you don't have a have a citrus orchard out back, you can still make your own home-freshening mix of potpourri. Even better, you can make lemonade, limeade, or orange juice, then slice up the remainder of the fruit. Lay the rind in slices on a big sheet pan and let them dry. Add dried rose petals, bunches of lilac, lavender, and rosemary, or mint for a wonderful, fresh scent. Tuck into muslin bags and tie up with a pretty and colorful ribbon, and you have a lovely all-occasion gift for housewarmings and holidays. Truly a blessing for any home.

> The only conclusion I have ever reached is that I love all trees, but I am in love with pines.
>
> **—Aldo Leopold**

BUTTERFLY HAVEN

If you want to increase the butterfly population in your yard, there's a wide variety of flowers that will attract them, including common yarrow, New York aster, Shasta daisy, coreopsis, horsemint, lavender, rosemary, thyme, butterfly bush, shrubby cinquefoil, common garden petunia, verbena, pincushion flowers, cosmos, zinnia, globe amaranth, purple coneflower, sunflowers, lupine, and delphinium. In creating a butterfly-friendly place, consider that they also need a wind protection, a quiet place to lay eggs, and water to drink.

If you want to see a butterfly garden before you get started, many botanical societies have them. In Washington, DC, the Smithsonian just opened one adjacent to the National Museum of Natural History. Good guides include: *The Butterfly Garden* by Mathew Tekulsky (Harvard Common Press) and *Butterfly Gardening* by Xerces Society/Smithsonian Institution (Sierra Club Books)

BUTTERFLY BUSH

There are somewhere around a hundred species of Buddleia, commonly referred to as the butterfly bush. The colorful flowers, ranging from white to pink, orange, and purple, attract an assortment of butterflies, including commas, mourning cloaks, sulphurs, monarchs, and several species of swallowtail.

MILKWEED

For those wanting to attract monarch butterflies to their gardens, nothing does the trick like planting milkweed, the host food plant for monarch caterpillars. Milkweed also attracts the viceroy, Baltimore checkerspot, mourning cloak, queen, great spangled fritillary, zabulon skipper, and question mark butterflies.

PARSLEY

A favorite among culinary herbs, parsley is a primary host food for the black swallowtail butterfly larva.

ALFALFA

Alfalfa is a host food for clouded yellow, orange sulphur, and Karner blue butterflies.

FENNEL

Also known as sweet anise, fennel is another favorite host food for many swallowtail caterpillars.

CLOVER

Common white or red clover will attract a whole host of butterflies to your garden, including common checkered skippers, painted ladies, buckeyes, sulphurs, gray hairstreaks, sleepy orange, eastern tailed-blue, silver-spotted skipper, and variegated fritillary.

VERBENA

Sulphurs and zebra longwings will be drawn to the nectar of most species of verbena.

QUEEN ANNE'S LACE

Another beautiful and easy-to-grow flowering herb, Queen Anne's lace is a host food for the anise swallowtail.

DAISY

Most varieties of daisy are favorite nectaring flowers for mourning cloak and queen butterflies. Daisies are also a host food for painted lady caterpillars.

HOLLYHOCK

Alcea, commonly known as hollyhock, is a host food for painted lady, checkered skipper, and gray hairstreak larva.

GOLDENROD

Flowers in the genus Solidago, known collectively as goldenrods, are a favorite nectar source for a variety of butterflies, including sulphurs, American snouts, red admirals, gorgone checkerspots, and viceroys.

DOGWOOD

Flowers of the dogwood tree attract spring azure and American snout butterflies. The leaves are also a host food for spring azure larva.

POPLAR

Most often planted as a fast-growing shade tree, poplars are also a host food for white admiral, tiger swallowtail, mourning cloak, viceroy, and red-spotted purple butterfly larva.

SNAPDRAGON

Plants of the genus Antirrhinum, collectively known as snapdragons, are host food for the larva of the common buckeye.

PURPLE CONEFLOWER

Echinacea purpurea, the purple coneflower, is well-known for its immune-boosting and anti-depressant properties. It is also an attractant for the common wood-nymph butterfly.

MUSTARD

Not only great for harvesting its seeds and greens for culinary use, the mustard plant is also a favorite nectaring and host food for falcate orangetip butterflies and larva.

PASSION VINE

Passiflora, also known as the passion vine, sports large, exotic purple flowers that will spice up any garden. The foliage is also a host food for gulf fritillary and zebra longwing caterpillars.

SUNFLOWER

In addition to providing sunflower seeds for human consumption, these summertime favorites provide nectar and host food for most species of checkerspot butterflies and larva.

VIBURNUM

A popular landscaping shrub due to its pleasant fragrance, viburnum will also attract Baltimore checkerspots and spring azure butterflies to your garden.

BURDOCK

Traditionally cultivated for the medicinal properties of its root, burdock is a favorite host food for painted lady caterpillars.

VETCH

A flowering plant of the legume family, any of the over a hundred species of vetch will attract American painted ladies, sulphurs, and zabulon skippers, as both a nectaring and larva host food source.

BLUEBERRY

These popular fruit-bearing bushes will bring both swallowtails and spring azure butterflies to your garden.

BLACK WALNUT

Juglans nigera, the black walnut tree, is host food for over two hundred species of butterfly and moth larvae, including swallowtails, red-spotted purples, royal walnut moths, and the elusive and exotic luna moth!

STONECROP

The name given to a variety of low-growing succulents, stonecrop is a favorite nectaring plant for the red admiral butterfly.

PRIVET

Finally, to create privacy in your butterfly garden, try surrounding the space with privet. The flowers of this hedge-forming shrub are a favorite for many butterflies, including skippers, painted ladies, swallowtails, and red-spotted purples.

PUBLIC GARDENING

Longing for a garden but have no place for one? Take advantage of the variety of places that have gardens: zoos, public gardens and parks, cemeteries, college campuses, garden club tours, nurseries and garden centers, or a friend's house. In many cities these days, there are also community gardens and gardening co-ops in which you can get your hands dirty. Call your parks and recreation department. (All of the above are also great places to get ideas if you do have a garden.)

> I believe a leaf of grass is no less than the
> journey-work of the stars,
> And the pismire is equally perfect, and
> a grain of sand, and the egg of the wren,
> and the tree-toad is a chef-d'oeuvre for
> the highest,
> And the runny blackberry would
> adorn the parlors of heaven
> And the narrowest hinge in my hand
> puts to scorn all machinery,
> and the cow crunching with depress'd
> head surpasses any statue,
> and a mouse is miracle enough to
> stagger sextillions of infidels
>
> —Walt Whitman

WITH FAMILY AND FRIENDS

> All God's pleasures are simple, the rapture of a May morning sunshine, the stream blue and green, kind words, benevolent acts, the glow of good humor.
>
> —F. W. Robertson

Going Wild for Wildflowers

My mother is a naturalist at heart. She treasures wildflowers much more than the domesticated plants I adopted as a child. She would take me on wildflower walks and teach me the secret flora of meadow and wood. I learned to identify wild irises, jack-in-the-pulpit,

Dutchman's breeches, larkspur, lady's slippers, and dozens of gorgeous and delicate specimens. I wondered at the difference between the small and seemingly rare wildflowers and the big and bold flowers that grew in our garden. The irises especially were in great contrast—wild irises were about four inches high and the irises I started from my aunt's were over two feet tall.

One day I decided to surprise my mother by transplanting some of her treasured wild irises to a flower bed at home. She was pleased, but warned me that these delicate plants simply wouldn't thrive outside their habitat. By the next spring, however, we had hearty clump of wild irises growing beside the shameless "flags" from Auntie's house.

> They tell us that plants are perishable, soulless creatures, that only man is immortal, but this, I think, is something that we know very nearly nothing about.
>
> —John Muir

BRINGING THE WOODS HOME

There are a number of woodland flowers that will do well in any shaded and treed part of your yard with moist, well-drained, rich-in-humus soil (you can add your own peat moss if you need to). These include lily of the valley (my personal favorite), dog's tooth violet, great trillium, red trillium, false Solomon's seal, Virginia bluebells, and redwood sorrel. But beware—don't go digging up plants in the woods: many, such as lady's slipper and swamp pink, are endangered. Better to get them from a reputable (some suppliers of difficult-to-propagate plants are over-collecting from the wild) company such as Prairie Moon Nursery (send two dollars to Rt. 2, Box 163, Winona, MN 53987 for a catalog) or Underwood Shade Gardens (508-222-2164, four dollars for a catalog).

> Each flower is a soul opening to nature.
>
> —Gerard de Nerval

SPRING DAY SACHET

This craft is delightfully easy to make and is a sweet and thoughtful gift!

- ½ yard lace
- 1 dinner plate
- disappearing ink marker
- scissors
- 1 cereal bowl
- tapestry needle

- **2 yards ¼″ wide ribbon**
- **2 ounces lavender or potpourri**
- **2 yards of inch-wide ribbon**

Place the lace on a table and lay the dinner plate on top of it. Trace the edge of the plate with the disappearing ink marker. Remove the plate and cut around marker to make a circle of lace. Turn the cereal bowl upside down in the center of the lace circle and trace the edge. Remove bowl. Thread the tapestry needle with the thin ribbon and stitch around the inner circle you have just created. (The size of stitches doesn't matter.) Tug gently on the ribbon so the lace gathers to make a pocket. When the opening is the size of a silver dollar, pour the lavender or potpourri in until full (about the size of a walnut). Tug the ribbon tight, tie in a knot, and cut the ends short. Tie the wide ribbon into a beautiful bow. Repeat until materials are gone.

Makes five sachets.

SEEDS OF WONDER

Kids love to help in the garden. It's a wonderful place for a child to learn and have fun and to spend enjoyable time with you. As you are starting to prepare your garden this spring, consider setting aside a special plot or container specifically for them. Pick plants that will grow quickly (patience is short) and those that have personality (like the face in a pansy); fragrance; texture (like lamb's ears); vibrant color; and/or attract butterflies. Good options depending on space and climate are: Chinese lantern, columbine, pinks, poppies, stock, sunflower, cornflower, bachelor's button, cosmos, violas, snapdragons, and zinnias. Take the kids with you to the nursery, and let them select from the above choices.

You can also help youngsters sprout seeds indoors. Fold a couple of paper towels together to form a strip as wide as the towel, around eighteen inches, and five inches high. Moisten and place inside a peanut butter jar or similar-size jar, forming a border at the base. Crumple and moisten another paper towel and stuff into the center. Carefully place seeds—beans are easy to grow and handle—between the folded paper and the glass. Keep moist, but not soaked, for several days as seeds germinate. Kids can watch roots and plants sprout. When plants reach above the jar and two sets of leaves have formed, transplant to pots of soil or into the ground.

> Every happening, great and small, is a parable whereby God speaks to us and the art of life is to get the message.
>
> —Malcolm Muggeridge

HEARTFUL GREENS

One easy way to entice your child into the garden is to make a patch with their name. Simply trace out his or her name in the loose soil and trace a big heart around it. Then plant a variety of fast-growing greens (leaf lettuce, radishes, watercress, arugula) in the furrows made by your tracings, water, and wait for his or her name and a big green heart to appear. Chances are your little ones will not only enjoy helping, but they will want to eat salad too!

> I have always thought a kitchen garden a more pleasant sight than the finest orangery or artificial greenhouse.
>
> —Joseph Addison

MAKING MAY BASKETS

When I was young, my brother and sister and I used to make May baskets for all the houses in the neighborhood to celebrate May Day. They were incredibly easy to make, and we would get such a thrill out of hanging them on front doorknobs, then ringing the bell and running to a hiding spot where we would observe the face of the recipient. It was then I first learned the particular pleasure of anonymous giving.

To make yourself or your neighbors a May basket, gather flowers (we always picked the first wild flowers of the season, but store-bought are okay too) and make them into an attractive bouquet. Tie the stems together with a rubber band. Moisten half a paper towel with water and wrap around the ends of the stem, then place a small plastic bag around the towel and tie with another rubber band. (This is to keep flowers fresh.) Set aside.

To make a cone basket, get an 8 ½ x 11-inch piece of construction paper. Hold the paper upright in two hands, as if you were reading a letter. Turn slightly so that the left corner points down at you. This will be the bottom of the cone. Roll one side so that it is tighter at bottom and more open at the top. Stick your hand in the top to expand the top opening and at the same time tighten the point at the bottom. Staple or tape the outer flap. When you finish, it should look like an waffle-type ice-cream cone. To make the handle, simply cut a half-inch wide strip from the long side of an 8 ½ x 11-inch piece of construction paper. Staple one end to each side of the cone. (You can also use ribbon or raffia if you want to.) Place flowers inside and you are ready to make your delivery!

> The garden is a love song, a duet between a human being and Mother Nature.
>
> —Jeff Cox

PLANT PASSALONGS

My husband and I both have green thumbs, and it can get to be somewhat of a problem. Our houseplants never die, and we are constantly having to pinch and hack them back. We feel guilty just throwing all those potential new plants into the compost, so we are always running out of room. I take plants into the office, but that's also getting overpopulated.

Recently, however, we have come across several non-plant people eager to get started and therefore happy to take a number of cuttings off our hands. Most of these folks are young (probably because you are either a plant person or not). We've given them as college graduation presents, first house presents, and new relationship presents. We always include fertilizer and instructions, and we always try to give plants appropriate to the light levels in the person's abode. Because this was a great solution to a "problem" of ours, it's been surprising to realize how pleasurable it is to start someone off on an interest in plants. They seem so happy; I recall my own first houseplant forays, and I'm left with a satisfied glow that no other gift-giving has ever provided.

> The music of the night insects has been familiar to every generation of men since the earliest humans; it has come down like a Greek chorus chanting around the actors throughout the course of human history.
>
> **—Edwin Way Teale**

THE ART OF PLANT PROPAGATION

Early spring is the best time to make new houseplants. There are four ways that plants propagate, ranging from easy to hard (I for one refuse to do air layering), and some plants respond only to one or the other.

1. Division: You just take a plant out of the pot, divide it into two or more clumps, roots and all, and replant into two or more pots. Plants that do well with this method include African violets, wax begonias, most ferns, agapanthus, and many orchids.
2. Offshoots and runners: Plants such as spider plant, strawberry geranium, and mother fern create ready-made babies, complete with tiny roots, as appendages that are considered runners. Bromeliads, clivias, and piggyback plants' offspring grow adjacent to the mother. In either case, I just detach the baby and plant it in a tiny pot out of direct sun, giving it plenty of moisture. (With runners, there's a way to do it while it is still attached to the plant, but that's too much work for me.)
3. Stem cuttings: My mainstay. Simply cut off a stem, strip off lower leaves, and place in water. (Don't touch the surface of the cut—bacteria from your skin can make the stem rot.) In a month or so, it will have rooted, and you can transplant it into a pot. Avoid rot by placing a couple of charcoal chips in the bottom of the container. Many houseplants will root this way, including coleus, fuchsia, philodendron, Swedish ivy, miniature rose, pothos, and wandering Jew. For cactus and succulents, let the cuttings dry for at least twenty-four hours, and root in rooting medium such as perlite or vermiculite.
4. Air layering: Required for dieffenbachia, dracaena, ficus, and split-leaf philodendron. To find out how to do this, ask at your local nursery.

> Flowers preach to us if we will hear.
>
> **—Christina Rossetti**

PLANT SWAPPING

Usually, passing along plants is a two-person exchange, but it is possible to set up a larger-scale swap. You could perhaps do it through your local agricultural co-op or set something up like a flea market or garage sale. Run an ad in the classifieds and tell all the garden club people in your community. I know of one group in Texas that had two hundred people show up! All you need are tables and a few rules. Here's how the Texas folks do it: They hold it in a place that can stand the dirt, require that donated plant be a "good" one—no unrooted cuttings, seeds, diseased plants, etc.—and limit the number of plants you can bring to swap. They ask people to label the plants they bring and include care instructions (Sun? Perennial? Drought-tolerant? Indoor?) As people bring in plants, each plant is given a number and a corresponding slip of paper with the same number goes into a hat. Then the hat is passed around and you get the plant with the number you draw. After that, people mill around trying to trade, if they don't like their plants, or get cuttings from the plants they lust after. If you have a smaller crowd, of course you can just have people barter between themselves for the plants they want and skip the numbers. Either way, the purpose is to have fun, mingle with plant people, and go home with something new.

> And this our life, exempt from public haunt Finds tongues in trees, books in running brooks, Sermons in stones and good in every thing.
>
> —William Shakespeare

INTO THE KITCHEN

> Everything is good in its season.
>
> —Italian proverb

Easy-Does-It Asparagus

The ancients believed that asparagus was an aphrodisiac. It certainly tastes good enough to be, but even if it isn't, the prospect of your own tender shoots each spring should entice you enough to give it a try in your garden. It takes about three years to get enough asparagus to make planting it worthwhile, but a maintained asparagus bed will last for twenty years, so you'll get plenty of spears for your efforts. While asparagus prefers cold winters, it will grow just about anywhere in the US. The trick is to dig a one-foot-deep trench and half-fill it with compost and ¼ cup bone meal per foot of trench. Plant roots eighteen inches apart, and don't fill in trench with dirt until roots begin to sprout.

> Green fingers are the extensions of a verdant heart.
>
> —Russell Page

Stir-Fried Asparagus

Once you've grown them and had your fill of them steamed, give this a try. It is delicious!

- 2 tablespoons low-sodium soy sauce
- 1 tablespoon dry sherry
- 1 tablespoon water or chicken broth
- 1 ½ pounds asparagus, ends snapped, and cut into small pieces
- 1 tablespoon sesame oil
- 2 teaspoons minced garlic
- 2 teaspoons minced fresh ginger
- ½ minced fresh basil
- ½ teaspoon sugar

Combine the soy sauce, sherry, and water or broth and set aside. Place a large (at least twelve-inch) skillet over high heat for 4 minutes. Add 2 teaspoons of the oil and heat for 1 minute or until the oil just starts to smoke. Add the asparagus and stir-fry for 2 minutes or until barely tender. Clear the center of the pan, add the garlic, ginger, and 1 teaspoon of oil, and sauté for 10 seconds. Remove pan from heat and stir the ingredients to combine.

Place pan back on heat, stir in the soy sauce mixture, and cook for 30 seconds. Add basil and sugar and cook for another 30 seconds. Serves four.

A HUMBLE ROOT

In his book, *Tomato Blessings and Radish Teachings*, Zen cleric and teacher Edward Espe Brown ruminates on the lessons food has to offer. Here he is attending a dinner party and describes the appetizer. "Radishes! Seated at a low table, we come face to face with platters of radishes, brilliantly red and curvaceous, some elongated and white-tipped, rootlets intact with topknots of green leaves sprouting from the opposite end. It was love at first sight. Gazing at the plentitude of radishes, red and round with narrow roots and spreading stems, I felt a swirling joy… These radishes kept growing on me, as if they exuded happiness… To be able to see the virtue, to appreciate the goodness of simple, unadorned ingredients—this is probably the primary task of the cook."

> Sow the living part of yourselves in the furrow of life.
>
> —Miguel de Unamino

WHEN IN PROVENCE: FABULOUS FRESH HERB SALAD

This is a salad from Provence that uses an unusual variety of late-spring greens and herbs.

- **One garlic clove, halved**
- **2 teaspoons lemon juice**
- **¼ teaspoons salt**
- **4 teaspoons olive oil**
- **1 teaspoon hot water**
- **4 cups arugula**
- **1–2 cups watercress, large stems removed**
- **1 ½ cups escarole**
- **¼ cup parsley, stems removed**
- **½ cup curly endive**
- **¼ cups small basil leaves**
- **20 small tarragon leaves**
- **10 small sage leaves**
- **5 chives, minced**
- **Pepper**

Rub the garlic clove halves all over a large wooden salad bowl. Whisk in the lemon, salt, all of the oil, and the water. Add greens and pepper to taste. Serve immediately. Serves four.

UNEXPECTED FRIENDS: VOLUNTEER VEGGIES

My city-born husband was at my Southern mother's house with me one year when she remarked that she felt like cooking a pot of "volunteers." After enjoying his confused expression for a few seconds, I explained that this is what she calls this small patch of turnip greens that come up every year without any coaching or invitation. So we headed out to pick a mess of them, and I schooled him on how to pick the small tender leaves, and to pick quickly so as to avoid the scratchy texture of the plants. He didn't care much for the greens, but I do think he enjoyed the picking.

> Anywhere you live you can find room for a garden somewhere.
>
> —**Jamie Jobb**

SUPERFOOD GARDEN GREENS

Besides turnip greens, there are many other vegetables that seem to be overlooked in the typical American diet. Recent research comparing French and American diets found that the French eat three times the variety of vegetables that we do, and the variety alone may have healthful benefits. So why not consider the following for your garden this summer?

- **Chard:** red or green, can be eaten raw when the leaves are tender, or used like cabbage to make chard rolls. Also good for a winter pasta sauce.
- **Kale:** member of cabbage family, popular among Romans and Greeks, loaded with vitamins and never bitter. Superb steamed.
- **Kohlrabi:** turnip-like root with edible stems. Can be eaten raw like an apple, shredded like a cabbage, or cooked like a turnip.
- **Amaranth:** also known as Chinese spinach. Rich in iron, calcium, vitamin A. Cooks like spinach or chard.
- **Good King Henry:** also known as poor man's asparagus. Leaves can be cooked like spinach.
- **Purslane:** can be used in salads or cooked like spinach. Sharp-tasting, but high in vitamin C and omega-3 fatty acids that help prevent heart problems.

TEA IN THE GARDEN: HOW TO MAKE COMPOST TEA

Compost tea is a marvelous way to feed your plants and give them extra nutrients in a wholly natural way that is free of chemicals. You want to feed your friends and family only the cleanest and pesticide-free produce, so start out organic and you will have a garden that produces healthy food. You will need a big bucket and the following to make compost tea:

- 2 cups homemade, fresh compost dirt
- 1 gallon of clean, filtered water

Add the water and the soil to a gallon bucket and keep in a place out of direct heat or cold; I use my outdoor shed, but a garage will also do nicely. Let your compost tea "brew" for a week and give it a stir every other day. Watering cans are the perfect teapot for your garden. Strain out the dirt and pour the liquid into your watering can, where it is ready to serve up some serious nutrients to your garden.

POPPING FRESH

You can grow your own popping corn. One of the most exotic varieties is pretty pops, which has kernels of red, blue, orange, black, purple, and yellow. Left on the cob, it's great for decorating your home. And it tastes wonderful when popped (the kernels turn white, though).

> It's the leisure hours, happily used, that have opened up a new world to many a person.
>
> **—George M. Adams**

RED-HOT ANTIOXIDANTS

If you like spicy food, consider growing a variety of hot peppers in the summer. Recently, scientists have found the substance that creates the heat in peppers. It's called capsaicin, an antioxidant that gives chilies their bite and, like all antioxidants, may help prevent cancer.

Some chili peppers, rated from low to high capsaicin content (and therefore amount of heat), are:

- New Mexico red: (rated 2–3)
- Jalapeno: 5
- Serrano: 6
- Tabasco: 8
- Thai: 9
- Scotch Bonnet: 10
- Savina: 10+

> There's something about sun and soil that heals broken bodies and jangled nerves.
>
> —Nature Magazine

GARDEN IN A JAR

The very first garden I remember was a sweet potato in a jar. My mama planted it when we were living in three tiny rooms behind our dress shop. There was no yard, no room outside even for a flowerpot. But Mama filled a Mason jar with water, propped the long, skinny sweet potato up in the glass with a trio of toothpicks, and told my brother and me to watch. By summer, the kitchen window was curtained with graceful vines and big curving leaves. And somehow that window garden made our shabby little kitchen into a special place. Even the light seemed different—more restful, more alive. That was when I first realized I needed a garden in my life.

> What I know of the divine sciences and the holy scriptures, I learned in the woods and fields. I have no other masters than the beeches and the oaks.
>
> —St. Bernard of Clairvaux

COMFREY FOR COMFORT

Comfrey is beloved by healers and is one of the best-known healing herbs of all time. It has even been referred to as "a one-herb pharmacy" for its inherent curative powers. Well-known and widely used by early Greeks and Romans, its very name, *symphytum*, from the Greek *symphyo*, means to "make grow together," referring to its traditional use of healing fractures. Comfrey relieves pain and inflammation. Comfrey salve will be a mainstay of your home first-aid kit. Use it on cuts, scrapes, rashes, sunburn, and almost any skin irritation. Comfrey salve can also bring comfort to aching arthritic joints and sore muscles.

Coconut-Comfrey Cure-All Salve

- ¾ cup comfrey-infused oil
- ¼ cup coconut oil
- 4 tablespoons beeswax
- 10 drops lavender essential oil

Combine comfrey and coconut oils. Heat the oil and wax together until the wax melts completely. Pour into a clean, dry jar. When the mixture has cooled a little, but has not yet set, add 10 drops of lavender essential oil, which is also an antiseptic. Seal the jar and store in a cabinet to use any time you scratch yourself working in the garden or want to renew and soften your hands and feet after a lot of house and yard work. One note: use it on the surface of your skin and it will work wonders, but, if a cut is deep, don't get it inside the wound. Let your physician handle that. Comfrey is a miracle plant for healing; in combination with the lavender, this power duo will restore your spirit along with your skin.

EMOTIONAL RESCUE REMEDY

Why does every day seem like it is weeklong nowadays? Unplugging from cable news and constant social media feeds will help, as will this time-tested aromatherapy healing potion. This remedy is an excellent way to recharge and refresh after a hectic week.

In a small ceramic or glass bowl, gently mix together the following essential oils with a small amount of base/carrier oil:

- **2 drops bergamot**
- **4 drops carrier oil (apricot or sesame, ideally)**
- **2 drops vanilla**
- **1 drop amber**
- **2 drops lavender**

Gently rub one drop of Calm Emotion Potion on each pulse point: on both wrists, behind your earlobes, on the base of your neck, and behind your knees. As the oil surrounds you with its warm scent, you will be filled with a quiet strength.

BEAUTIFYING YOUR HOME

> Now the earth with many flowers puts on her spring embroidery.
>
> —Sappho

Shabby Chic in the Garden

To add a distinctive look to outdoor plants pots and planters, try this simple trick. Create a mixture containing one part garden soil, two parts peat moss, and one part water—the mixture should be gooey and thick in consistency. Using a garden trowel or your hand, spread the exterior of a terra-cotta pot or planter with the mixture, and allow to dry. Sow seeds or outdoor plants plantings as desired in the pots, and water normally. Within a few weeks, the peat moss mixture will have blossomed with a variety of mosses and lichens, giving your pots a verdant, natural patina.

> Growing a garden and staying out in the fresh air after office hours seemed to give me the strength to meet all problems with greater courage.
>
> —Jim G. Brown

MINTCENSE

One thing you can do, if you decide to grow a variety of mint, is to make mint potpourri. Originally made in colonial times, when it was believed to "clear the head," it is an excellent natural room freshener.

- ¼ cup orris root
- 1 tablespoon oil of lavender or pennyroyal
- 2 cups dried orange mint
- 2 cups dried spearmint
- 2 cups dried peppermint
- 1 cup dried thyme
- 1 cup dried rosemary

Combine the orris root and essential oil. Add the rest of the ingredients and combine gently, taking care not to crush the leaves too much. Store it in a covered jar. To use, shake and open.

MOTHER NATURE'S MOTH REPELLENTS

If you want to avoid using mothballs for your woolens this coming summer, try dried branches of rue, tansy, mint, lavender, rosemary, pennyroyal, and wormwood, either by themselves or in combination. Tie them together and, to keep them from flaking onto your closet floor, wrap them lightly in cheesecloth and hang upside down from a ribbon in your closet.

> A house, though otherwise beautiful, yet if it hath no garden is more like a prison than a house.
>
> —William Coles

GO ORGANIC: EASTER EGGS WITH NATURAL DYES

Want to do something a little more sophisticated this Easter? You and your older kids might enjoy the subtle beauty of these natural wonders. But beware—these are for decoration only. Do not eat.

- 1 red cabbage
- 2 very large brown-skinned onions (a.k.a. yellow onions)
- 1 dozen eggs
- 36 rubber bands
- 2 dozen small fern fronds and/or fresh and dried flower blossoms
- 1 tablespoon powdered alum
- 1 roll cheesecloth

Without cutting the cabbage in two, cut the central core out and separate the leaves so that each leaf is as large as possible. Cut the two ends of the onions and peel the skin off, again keeping each piece of skin as large as possible.

Place a fern or flower against an egg, one on either side, and wrap it completely with a red cabbage leaf, using two rubber bands to keep it on. Repeat for five more eggs. Use the onion skins and remaining flowers and ferns for the other six eggs, again using two rubber bands to affix. Cut 12 pieces of cheesecloth, big enough to wrap completely around each egg, and secure with two more rubber bands.

Place the cabbage eggs in one pot and the onion eggs in another. Add water and 1 ½ teaspoon alum to each pot. Bring to a boil, reduce heat, and simmer for 15 minutes. Remove from heat and allow eggs to cool in water. Unwrap and enjoy your designs. Makes a dozen.

> The hours when the mind is absorbed by beauty are the only hours when we really live.
>
> **—Richard Jefferies**

EGGSHELL PLANTERS

Ordinary eggshells make beautiful planters for small herbs or grasses. Break raw eggs, leaving shell at least one-half intact. Empty the contents into a separate bowl, and rinse the shell thoroughly. Place already-sprouting plants (mint, lavender, chives, or sage work well, as will wheatgrass, alfalfa, or small ferns) in the shells, anchored with a bit of topsoil. Cushion an assortment of shells and plants in moss, and place in a beribboned basket or pot. Experiment using dyed or decorated eggshells.

WONDERFUL WATER GARDENS

It seems that garden ponds are in these days—the garden catalogs are full of such kits. I even have a friend who had an entire stream put into his property. I must say, when I saw it, I lusted after it myself until I realized the trouble and expense it would involve. One day I read an article by the horticulturalist for the Denver Botanic Gardens in which he sang the praises of tiny water gardens. They are easy to create, hard to goof on (you can always rearrange) and—as long you have a location that gets six hours of sun—the plants are hard to kill. So I decided to give it a try. Mine is made out of one of those nine-inch black plastic containers that look like they're cast iron. All it has is tiny cattail, a spider lily, and a clump of cranberry taro. It sits in the middle of my vegetable garden, and I smile every time I see it.

beets
spinach
blueberries
red cabbage
turmeric
onion skin

> To live happily is an inward power of the soul.
>
> —Marcus Aurelius

MAKE YOUR OWN MINI-POND

All it takes is a watertight container and a few plants. You can use half-barrels, if you line them with PVC liner (available at garden centers), or ceramic pots, as long as you seal them with two coats of sealant. Plastic pots require no preparation. Use plants with contrasting shapes to create an appealing design, but don't use too many different ones; you're working in a small space, and too much variety will look chaotic. And remember—they will grow, so take that into account in your design. You just submerge the pot, dirt and all, into the water. You can get height differentials by setting the plants on submerged bricks or overturned pots. Good water plants include water lettuce, water hyacinth, sweet flag, parrot feathers, cannas, calla lilies, giant arrowhead, yellow pitcher plant, and water celery. Fertilize with pellets available at any nursery. If you live in a place that freezes, bring the plants in to use as houseplants for the winter, or keep them in a tub of water in the basement. They most likely will need to be divided in the spring. Start another pond or give the new ones away.

> We are not sent into this world to do anything into which we cannot put our hearts.
>
> —John Ruskin

NOURISHING BODY AND SOUL

> My faith is all a doubtful thing,
> Wove on a doubtful loom,
> Until there comes, each showery spring
> A cherry tree in bloom.
>
> —David Morton

Elderflower Elegance: DIY Tonic

If you live in an area where elderflowers grow, here's an old-fashioned skin tonic. This is a great gift when packaged in a beautiful glass bottle decorated with an old botanical illustration of an elderflower. Be sure to include storage instructions.

- 50 elderflower heads, washed in cold water
- a 1-quart jar, sterilized
- 2 ½ cups water
- 5 tablespoons vodka
- cheesecloth
- decorative glass bottles with lids

Remove petals from heads, making sure not to bruise the flowers; do not include stems. Place petals in quart jar. Boil water and pour over flowers. Let stand for 30 minutes, and add vodka. Cover and let stand on counter for 24 hours. Pour liquid through cheesecloth into glass bottles and cap. Store in refrigerator until used, then keep in cool, dry, dark place, like a cabinet, and use within one month. Makes 3 cups.

WELCOME YOUR BACKYARD NEIGHBORS: GIVING BIRDS A HOME

Birds really do like birdhouses, as long as you make them hospitable. Make a birdhouse fit into its surroundings, both in color and texture, as much as possible (twigs, bark, and unpainted materials are best; birds don't want to feel on display).

Place any house at least six feet off the ground and away from foot and cat traffic. Face it away from the sun, preferably in trees or shrubs. Don't despair if a bird doesn't move in until the second year the house is there; they need time to get used to it. One easy bird-friendly option is to buy a standard birdhouse at a store and hot-glue straw or dried grasses to the roof, creating a natural thatched effect. For more elaborate handmade houses, consult *The Bird Feeder Book* by Tom Boswell (Lark Books) and the *Bird House Book* by Bruce Woods and David Schoonmaker (also Lark Books). Lark (800-284-3388) also has a number of birdhouse and bird feeder kits for sale.

> Birds are as important as plants in my garden.
>
> —Anne Scott-James

GROW YOUR OWN SPONGE

Did you know that you can grow your own loofah sponges? They are actually gourds (genus Luffa) and are available through many garden catalogs. Plant now and you can harvest next fall, not only for your family, but also to give as gifts. To use, let the gourd ripen on the vine (it turns from green to yellow as it ripens). But don't let it get fully yellow—slightly green means it will be a more tender sponge. When it's time to harvest, cut it off the vine, peel the skin like an orange, and let the gourd dry for about ten days. Then cut it open from the big end, remove the seeds by shaking, and strip off any remaining skin. Rinse the inside fibers and then submerge the sponge in water for 12 hours. Peel off the outside layer if any remains, and dry in the shade. If the sponge is too hard, you can soften it by boiling it in water for 5 minutes.

> No occupation is so delightful to me as the culture of the earth...and no culture comparable to that of the garden...but though an old man, I am but a young gardener.
>
> **—Thomas Jefferson**

SPRING CLEANING FOR BODY AND SOUL

You can give your skin a great spring cleaning with all-natural products.

For oily skin: Mix 1 egg white and 1 tablespoon of oatmeal. Apply in a thin layer to face and neck and leave on for 15 to 20 minutes. Egg white contains papain, a natural enzyme that eliminates subcutaneous dirt and oil: the oatmeal is rich in protein and potassium and will give your skin a vital mineral boost.

For dry skin: Spread a thin, even layer of honey on face and neck, taking care to avoid eyes. Honey is a natural humectant and traps moisture in the skin.

Homemade Alpha-Hydroxy Mask: Cook half of a diced and peeled apple in ¼ cup of milk until soft and tender. Mash, then cool to room temperature and apply to skin. Thoroughly cleanse with warm water after 15 to 20 minutes.

> I have always loved willows; they are the only trees who have wantonly escaped from the classic idea of a tree.
>
> —Katherine Butler Hathaway

GARDEN SURPRISES

Every spring, I make a trip to the nursery to load up on puny little plants that have no blooms. It's an act of faith, because half the time I have no idea what they'll look like. Then, in summer, the color combinations in my garden come as a wonderful surprise, far better than if I'd planned them. Gardening in spring is life-affirming. The outcome is often less important than the promise of things to be, and the plants transforming in my flower beds remind me of the potential for growth in other areas of my life.

SOUL-SOOTHING SOAK

If you suffer from aches and pains, you may find the following bath remedy to be soothing and calming. The water will dilate your blood vessels and relax your muscles, while the herbs provide aromatherapy.

- **3 tablespoons dried lavender**
- **2 tablespoons dried rose petals**
- **3 tablespoons dried chamomile**
- **2 tablespoons hops**

Combine the herbs in a glass or ceramic bowl and pour in a quart of boiling water. Cover and let set for an hour. Strain the herbs and pour the liquid under the running tap of a warm (not hot) bath.

A GOOD WORKOUT

Gardening is good exercise. If you rake, hoe, dig, or pull weeds by hand, you can burn up to three hundred calories per hour. The American Council on Exercise recommends that you do a brisk ten-minute walk before you start to warm up your body. Those with back problems (the most common gardening complaint) should take particular care to walk first. Back sufferers should also be careful about lifting—bend those knees! And you might want to consider a knee pad for hand weeding.

> I'd rather have roses on my table than diamonds on my neck.
>
> **—Emma Goldman**

MAKING THE MOST OF MINT

Be careful what you wish for when you plant mint. Be sure you like it, and be sure you like it everywhere! I have seen people try a variety of ways to contain its virulent spread throughout the garden, but the most ingenious was a woman who planted it in an old claw-foot bathtub. Her one word of caution—be sure to close the drain.

Besides peppermint, there is apple mint (also known as woolly mint), black peppermint, orange mint, pineapple mint, and spearmint. Each has its own distinct flavor; all have many different uses. When harvesting mint for cooking, use only the top three to five leaves of each branch; the lower leaves are too pungent. Here are a few ways to try minting up your life.

Marvelous Mint Foot Scrub

- 1 cup unflavored yogurt
- 1 cup of kosher or rock salt
- ¾ cup mint leaves

Combine ingredients and apply to feet. Use a damp washcloth to gently scrub rough spots. Rinse feet and apply a thick lotion or petroleum jelly.

Minty Facial Astringent

- 1 tablespoon fresh peppermint or spearmint
- 1 cup witch hazel

Combine ingredients in a jar with a tight-fitting lid. Steep in cool, dry place for one week, shaking occasionally. Strain and pour liquid into a bottle or spray bottle. Use about 1 teaspoon per day. Makes about a six-week supply.

> Life begins the day you start a garden.
>
> —Chinese proverb

CHAPTER TWO

Summer

What wondrous life is this I lead!
Ripe apples dropped about my head;
The luscious clusters of the vine
Upon my mouth do crush their wine;
The nectarine and curious peach
into my hands themselves do reach;
Stumbling on melons, as I pass,
Ensnared with flowers, I fall on grass.

—Andrew Marvell

IN THE GARDEN

> Summer afternoon—summer afternoon; to me, those have always been the two most beautiful words in the English language.
>
> —Edith Wharton

On a warm summer's day, the delightful scents of rosemary, mint, and lavender perfume the air as bees and hummingbirds go about their feeding. Perhaps you harvest a handful of lavender to scent your underwear drawer. Later, run out to snip some parsley and chives to add zest to a salad and throw together a bouquet of bright red bergamot and silvery artemisia for the dinner table. Or maybe today is the day you create fragrant potpourri and dried wreaths from the bounty of your garden to please the eyes and noses of friends and family.

Nothing is more pleasing, useful, and easy than growing an herb garden, even if you only have a tiny plot of land. You don't even really need a yard, because herbs can be easily grown in pots on a deck or terrace or even indoors, if you have a sunny window. If you do have an outdoor space, tuck herbs in the border of a flower garden or in a patch in the vegetable garden, or simply plant them outside the kitchen door, like they do in France, so you just lean outside when you want something. Because they are virtually indestructible, they are perfect for beginning gardeners. Most are fast-growing and pest-resistant. Chances are your only problem will be how quickly they spread; some can be quite invasive.

Choosing what to grow is a pleasure in and of itself. Think about what and how you cook, and whether you would like to make your own flower crafts and potpourris. Then pick accordingly. I personally hate to pay for a bunch of dill at the store because when I need it, I only want a little, and the rest always spoils in the fridge. So dill was at the top of my list. Some other common culinary herbs to consider: basil, chives, marjoram, mint, parsley, sage, rosemary, thyme, savory, cumin, and oregano. If you want a scented garden and plan to make bouquets, potpourris, wreaths, etc., you might want to plant bergamot (beautiful shaggy red flowers), dyer's chamomile, lady's mantle, lamb's ears, lavender, lemon balm, lemon verbena, nasturtiums, rue, santolina, tansy, violets, woodruff, and yarrow.

> Here are the sweet peas, on tiptoe for a flight...
>
> —John Keats

Four O'Clocks

Some flowers are pure magic. I first learned that when I got the packet of flower seeds for a 4-H project one spring. The flowers were called four o'clocks and, as evidenced by the brightly colored picture on the front, were quite showy. I eagerly dug up a bed in front of my house and sowed the seeds in wobbly rows. Every day, I ran out to check on the progress, which, of course, because I was an impatient eight-year-old, wasn't quick enough for me.

Finally, after an agonizing couple of weeks, the seedlings came poking through. They grew pretty rapidly—those that could survive my overwatering. I must confess that I had gotten bored with the plain green seedlings; then the first flower buds appeared. They all burst into bloom on practically the same day, filling the front of my house with a riot of color. I, too, was bursting with pride and made all of my family and neighbors look at the amazing miracle the seed packet had produced. By the time I had rounded everybody up, however, the flowers were closed up tightly. Every one of them! That's why they're called four o'clocks, my mother explained. Every day they close up at 4:00 sharp and open up with the first rays of sun in the morning. I checked every day, and she was right. Four o'clock sharp. You can set your watch by my flowers!

> Flowers are sunshine, food, and medicine to the soul.
>
> **—Luther Burbank**

HERBAL INCENSE: NATURAL ENERGY CLEANSER

Sweetgrass: Native Americans have burned braided sheaves of sweetgrass for centuries. It is so aromatic, it can also be wafted around as a wand to clear energy without lighting it. Native folks also brew a tea from it to use as an astringent body and hair rinse and as an adornment, woven into braids or crowns. They go by the philosophy that "strong hair means a strong mind." This power herb cleanses body, soul, and your home; however, its highest use is for rituals, as it can be burned to call forth the ancestors and send away anything unwanted.

Copal: Mexican and South American tribal healers and modern shamans gather this tree resin to employ as ceremonial incense throughout the year. You will smell the sweetly pungent smoke of copal on the Day of the Dead, as it helps us connect with our ancestors and loved ones who have passed to the other side. While burning it is part of the ritual, it is also believed by shamans and healers to help one tap into the spiritual realm. Copal also has the power to bring about total relaxation.

Palo Santo: This dried wood plays an important role in South American cultures, where it is burned to clear a space of bad energy. It also activates a higher power in those who use it. The scent of Palo Santo clears out psychic clutter and purifies both you and your environment. It is said to literally burn away negative thoughts in your mind, a deeply powerful experience.

> All is miracle. The stupendous order of nature, the revolution of a hundred million worlds around a million suns, the activity of light, the life of animals, all are grand and perpetual miracles.
>
> —Voltaire

EFFORTLESS HERBS: ROSEMARY, OREGANO, MINT, CHIVES, AND SAGE

Sage is a marvelous cooking herb and is truly easy to grow. Sage doesn't like is wet ground, so plant it in a sunny spot with rich, well-drained soil. There are several sage varieties to choose from, including some with colored leaves. Harvest the leaves regularly to encourage more to grow. This versatile herb is not only a culinary pleasure but is also very important in your magic.

Parsley is the gift that gives for two years. This herb can be slow to germinate; try soaking the seeds in water overnight before planting to speed it up. The best place to grow parsley is in rich, moist soil in full sun or partial shade.

Oregano loves a Mediterranean clime. Plant yours in warm, sunny spots with light soil. Oregano has pretty pink flowers and makes great ground cover at the front of borders. Don't allow this herb to get too tall—make sure to pinch it back and you'll get more of this tasty treat to harvest.

Mint is a marvel. It spreads beautifully once it has really taken root. If space is a concern, plant your mint in pots to contain the roots and keep it from taking over. Keep it in full sun or partial shade and pinch out any flower buds to encourage more leaf growth.

Thyme is a cousin of mint and grows much lower to the ground; it is one of the most fragrant of herbs and really adds flavor as a culinary herb. Plant this to remove melancholy from your home and garden. If your front yard and door get afternoon sun, plant woolly thyme and you'll come home after work to a perfume paradise that immediately lends cheer and comfort.

Coriander is a very versatile herb for the kitchen and grows well in the garden or in pots. Seeds can take weeks to germinate and the plants are fairly short-lived, so sow seeds every few weeks to get you through the season. Coriander is a bit fussy and can "bolt" when stressed, which means it produces flowers and seeds and not enough of the flavorful leaves. You need to make sure it is well-watered, and reap regularly before it goes to seed.

Rosemary is useful for so many culinary and magical means. Luckily for us, it grows vigorously. Rosemary can be trimmed in early summer to keep it in shape and stop it getting too woody.

Basil is beloved because it's so delectable and versatile. It is easily grown in pots. Take care to remove the growing tip when the plants are six inches (fifteen cm) high for bushier growth. Plant out in the garden when the weather gets warmer. Basil prefers full sun.

Chives come from the onion family and have slim, pointed leaves. You should sow seeds directly in the ground in early spring, late March or April. Chives grow best in a sunny spot with rich soil, so keep the plants watered. Chives produce pretty purple or pink, perfectly round flowers. Gorgeous in the garden and palatable on the plate.

All of these herbs will grow happily in containers on a patio or balcony, and even on the kitchen windowsill. Start an herb garden this year and you'll never look back.

SCENT OF SERENITY LAVENDER MIST

My Aunt Edith, who introduced me to the wonders of gardening, had a linen closet that always smelled sweetly of lavender. I remember breathing in the smell and immediately feeling comforted. Sleeping on crisp, clean, herb-scented sheets always made for the soundest sleep and most delicious dreams. (Little did I know at the time, lavender is also a moth repellent and an adaptogen, adjusting to satisfy your own energy needs.) Here is a potion for dreamers:

- 4 drops lavender oil
- 3 drops chamomile oil
- 3 drops orange oil
- 4 ounces distilled spring water

Shake the oils and water in a colored-glass spray bottle or mister.

Fifteen minutes before you retire, spray your bed linens, bath towel, pillow, and all around your room. You may want to keep a dream journal by your bed to record what happens during the night.

Imbued with Love: Lavender Rosemary-Infused Vodka

This clear alcoholic drink is also easily infused with the flavor of flowers, herbs, fruits, and even vegetables. Try combinations, such as the light and sweet floral taste of lavender and rosemary. Lavender brings calm and healing, and rosemary dispels negative spirits. Both of these are love herbs. What could be better? You'll need the following:

- A quart bottle of vodka
- 2 sprigs of rosemary
- 3 sprigs of lavender
- Larger Mason canning jar with sealable lid

After you have rinsed your herbs in cool water and gently patted them dry, put them in the 1-quart (32-ounce) Mason jar. Pour in vodka, making sure to cover the herbs to the top, and seal tightly. Give a vigorous shake and place in your pantry or dark closet for five days, making sure to shake at least once a day. After the second day, take a spoon and taste the vodka. If the taste suits you before the full five days are up, go ahead and strain the herbs out using cheesecloth or a paper coffee filter. Set the herbs aside and let them dry. After the vodka is thoroughly strained of any herbs or residue, pour it into a bottle, and label it with the date and the herbs. Tie the dry herbs into a bundle with string and use when you next make a fire in the hearth. The aromatic smoke will imbue your home with coziness, calm, healing, and love.

LAZY SUMMER DAYS

I can't possibly count the hundreds of summer hours I used to spend in the fields around my parents' house, lying in the tall grass, the hot sun beating down, the smell of green strong in the air. I was mostly alone, searching for butterflies and dragonflies, making daisy and clover chains, just whiling away the hours. A friend and I would pick buttercups and hold them under one another's chins to see if we liked butter and pull petals off daisies to find out who the boy down the street favored: "He loves me, he loves me not." It was forty years ago, but the rush of memories comes flooding back. And I mourn for the lost fields, all covered in houses now, and the lost freedom of children now, who must be supervised and shepherded wherever they go.

> Ah, summer, what power you have to make us suffer and like it.
>
> **—Russell Baker**

GARDEN YOUR WAY TO GLADNESS

For dispelling negative energy, plant heather, hawthorn, holly, hyacinth, hyssop, ivy, juniper, periwinkle, and nasturtiums.

For healing, plant sage, wood sorrel, carnation, onion, garlic, peppermint, and rosemary.

Farming and working with plants are guided by the moon and should take place during the waxing moon in the signs of Cancer, Scorpio, Pisces, Capricorn and Taurus.

INVITE FRIENDLY FAIRIES INTO YOUR GARDEN: OPEN A FAIRY DOOR

I don't know about you, but wood saws scare me a bit, and I am much more comfortable constructing with glue. I live in the San Francisco Bay Area, where fairy doors are a "a thing" and the island of Alameda has more of these delights than any other neighborhood. So much inspiration, and I feel in love with some fancy fairy doors that were made very simply from popsicle sticks and adorned with crystals, glitter, lovely paint, and all manner of décor. Gather the kids as this is tons of fun for the family! Fairy garden doors are very easy to make and you can get really creative with them.

Start by buying popsicle sticks, which are easily available at any craft store or larger grocery stores. I get mine from JoAnn Fabrics, where you can also get lots of beads, glitter, good glue, and here is my big secret weapon—glitter nail polish from the Dollar Store! After my first two, a "fairy door shoebox," filled with tools and goodies, was a necessity. Gorilla Glue is best if you plan to keep your fairy doors outside all year; it can withstand rain, snow, freezing temperatures, and even a lot of visits from the wee ones themselves.

Fairy Garden Doors: Construction

Lay popsicle sticks out to create the design you want. Cut two cross-pieces to hold it all together and glue. I used a box cutter to cut the pieces. You probably can get away with using a good pair of scissors or a sharp cooking knife. Be careful, of course, and if kids are involved, do the cutting for them. Decide on your color scheme, and you can either stain with a wood stain or use the recipe for organic flour paint in this book. I love using the brightly colored and glitter nail polish on my most lavish fairy doors. Once the paint or stain is dry, pick out cool buttons, charms, or rhinestones from old jewelry, and faux moss (the Dollar Store's is a very affordable choice), and glue it on. The only rule for creating this sweetest of garden crafts is to have as much fun as possible and share the experience with the ones you love.

Fairy Flora

When planting your garden of enchantments, bear in mind that certain plants attract hummingbirds, butterflies, and fairies. The wee folk love daisies, purple coneflower, French lavender, rosemary, thyme, yarrow, lilac, cosmos, red valerian, sunflowers, honeysuckle, and heliotrope. Folk wisdom handed down through the centuries claims that pansies, blue columbine, and snapdragons planted in beds are a welcome mat for fairies and that they can use foxglove, which means "folk's glove," to make hats and clothing, as well as tulips for their haberdashery. They also favor sunny-faced nasturtiums. Fairies are also quite attached to certain fruit trees, with pear, cherry, and apple being their absolute favorites. The hawthorn is one of the most magical trees. It marks the fairies' favorite dancing places, and you should not cut or uproot a hawthorn unless you wish to incur their wrath. Keep your eyes peeled when these trees are in bloom, as there are bound to be fairy folk about!

ODE TO MORNING GLORIES

I have realized anew the almost spiritual beauty of the common morning glory. I avoided planting these flowers anywhere about the garden, because they seed so freely that they soon become an annoyance, strangling more important plants and even mischievously tangling up the vegetables. Instead, I have given them a screen that breaks the bareness of the tool house, and let them run riot. The leaves are not especially notable, being rather coarse, but the flowers are as exquisite in their richly colored fragility as if Aurora, in the bath, had amused herself by blowing bubbles. These, catching the sunrise glow, floated away upon the breeze and, falling on a wayside vine, opened into flowers that from their origin vanish again under the sun's caress.

Among all their colors, none is more beautiful or unusual than the rich purple with the ruddy throat merging to white—night shadows melting into the clear light of dawn.

> The earth laughs in flowers.
>
> **—Ralph Waldo Emerson**

IONS AND EONS OF CONTENTMENT: SALT LAMP SERENITY

Your entryway is where things cross the threshold into your realm. Energy management starts right at the front door. One way to keep a constant vigil on this is by having a Himalayan salt lamp in the front room. Salt is one of Mother Nature's greatest protectors, as it cleanses your environment of ill omens and bad spirits. These lovely blocks of rosy-hued salt produce negative ions when warm—the very thing that makes a beach day by the ocean so cheering. A simple DIY way to have your negative ions and enjoy them, too, is to buy a batch of rock salt chunks at your nearby new age store or even a gourmet shop. Take a metal or wire bowl, place a small light bulb in the bottom center of the basket, and stack the rock salt over it. You'll immediately enjoy the gentle, soft pink glow of the light and, as the rocks warm up, your mood will begin to lift. As a double benefit, the salt will constantly cleanse the energy in your home and keep it light and bright.

> Awake, O north wind, and come thou south!
> Blow upon my garden, that the spices thereof may flow out.
>
> **—Song of Solomon**

BEAUTIFUL WEEDS

It's amazing how the variety of flowers and their availability changes throughout the United States. In the South I was used to a profusion of wildflowers—black-eyed Susans, sweet peas, Queen Ann's lace, daylilies—lining the roads and filling the fields; I picked freely, without consequence or expense, and our house never lacked a bouquet or two. I've never quite grown accustomed to life in San Francisco, where I have to actually pay for these same flowers at a florist or farmers' market. My mother laughed at me for buying Queen Ann's lace for my wedding bouquet. "Why do you want a weed in there?" she asked. And I realized that, through sheer geography, Queen Anne's lace has become a unique and beautiful flower to me that is worth every penny.

> June reared that bunch of flowers you carry,
> from seeds of April's sowing.
>
> —Robert Browning

CONFESSIONS OF A TOMATO GROWER

Some of my most sublime moments have been at four in the morning, when the irrigation water comes through. Alone, under a full moon, in the garden, you see subtle variations. Sometimes I look at the foliage of my tomatoes and think I would grow tomatoes even if they didn't grow fruit. It's like looking at the stars as your eyes become accustomed to the dark. First you see a thousand stars, then you see ten thousand.

> The cherry tomato is a wonderful invention, producing, as it does, a satisfactorily explosive squish when bitten.
>
> —Miss Manners

DON'T PANIC, GO ORGANIC!

You don't need a mass of chemical pesticides, weed killers, and fertilizers to have a lush garden. There are a number of things you can do to reduce the amount of chemicals on your fruit, vegetables, and flowers, which in turn will reduce the amount of such items in the water and air and limit exposure to birds, bees, butterflies, your children, and yourself. First, start a compost pile (see directions on page 138). It should eliminate your need for non-organic fertilizer. Ask your nursery about organic ways of fertilizing lawns; there are several. Learn about biological ways of controlling pests: praying mantises, spiders, and ladybugs reduce harmful insects. My only method of aphid control for two dozen rose bushes is to buy a batch of ladybugs at the beginning of the flowering season; it works like a charm. Ladybugs are available at most nurseries and through catalogs such as Plow & Hearth (which also has great things like butterfly sanctuaries and nesting birdhouses for sale); call 800-627-1712 for a catalog.

You can also plant flowers that attract beneficial insects. Good ones include all the daisies, plants in the carrot family (Queen Ann's lace, sweet alyssum, chervil, and caraway) and anything in the mint family, including basil and oregano (yup, they're mints too). And when choosing plants in the first place, consider how disease- and insect-resistant they are; for example, Tropicana roses attract more aphids than Angel Face.

There are all kinds of bug-deterring herbs that can be planted as companions to various vegetables and flowers: marigolds are the workhorse here; they deter most bugs. Garlic should be planted between rose bushes to keep away Japanese beetles. Basil repels flies and mosquitoes and helps tomatoes grow. Horseradish helps keep potato bugs away. Mint and peppermint deter white cabbage moths. Ask at your nursery for a complete list.

Decide how much damage you can live with and go for the highest-impact strategy—sometimes a strong blast with a garden hose will work wonders. Hot chilies are an effective insecticide. Chop up a few hot ones, mix with detergent and water, and spray on plants (you can add garlic and onion too for real kick). Or dust plants with ground chili pepper. There are also a number of very effective, yet harmless, herbal pesticides, including Ryania (used against aphids, Japanese beetles, and certain moths), white hellebore (good against slugs, caterpillars, and other leaf-munching pests), pyrethrum (effective against slugs), nicotine and derris (good for controlling aphids and caterpillars), and rotenone (good general insecticide, effective against fleas on pets).

If you must use chemicals, read the labels. Those labeled "Danger—Poison" should not be used by backyard gardeners; those labeled "Caution" are less dangerous and therefore less harmful. Soaps and oils are lower in toxicity than sprays and powders, and spot treatment is less harmful than broad-spectrum spraying. Never apply chemicals in the in the heat of the day or in the presence of children or pets, and make sure the garden has completely dried before letting kids or pets back outside. Store such items out of the reach of kids. To receive the Environmental Protection Agency's free pamphlets on the subject, call (800) 490-9198.

> When you can put your foot on seven daisies, summer is come.
>
> —Proverb

PRIDE OF PANTRY PICKLES: YOUR GARDEN IN A JAR

This is a recipe handed down from generation to generation in my family; my mother was very proud of and famous for her pickles. This same cucumber recipe can be used to pickle almost any vegetable: inkling onions, peppers, squash, baby corn, green tomatoes, cauliflower, and anything you might fancy. Your own home-grown dill will be a wonderful finishing touch. Gather:

- 3 dozen cucumbers (3 to 4 inches long)
- 3 cups water
- 3 cups vinegar
- 6 tablespoons kosher salt
- ½ to 1 clove garlic per jar, blanched and sliced
- 1 bunch fresh dill or ½ teaspoon dried dill per jar (you can use seed heads, leaves, and stems, too)
- ½ tablespoon mustard seed per jar
- 2 one-quart Mason canning jars (or six pint jars)

Wash all the cucumbers using cool water. In a big stock pot, pour in the vinegar, 3 cups of water, and kosher salt and bring to a boil. This is the brining liquid. In the bottom of a sterilized quart jar, place a generous layer of dill, a clove of garlic, and ½ tablespoon mustard seed. Pack the cucumbers vertically into the jar until it is about half full, then add another layer of dill and fill the remainder of the jar with cucumbers. Fill all the jars in the exact same way, leaving a half inch at the top for the brine. After you have poured in the brining liquid, go ahead and seal the Mason jars. Place the jars in a boiling-water bath for 15 minutes to sterilize your pickle jars. Label when your pickle jars have cooled and store on a cool, dark shelf for two weeks.

BUG-EATING BIRDS

Another way to eliminate the need for pesticides is to encourage your feathered friends to dine at your house. Here's how:

1. Place birdbaths throughout the garden, away from bushes that can hide cats. Keep them clean and filled with fresh water.
2. Create a fountain with trickling water; the sound and movement are attractive to birds.
3. Plant a diverse array of plants, particularly natives.
4. Don't use any chemicals on your garden, as they can kill birds.

For answers to all kinds of bird questions, you can call Cornell University's Laboratory of Ornithology (607-254-2473) or the National Audubon Society's Bird and Wildlife Information Center (212-979-3080, website www.audubon.org).

BEING PREPARED

I always keep a bucket filled with whatever tools I may need in my garden. I started this after years of saying, "Oh, that rose needs pruning; I'll go get my clippers" or "That tomato needs staking. I'll do it tomorrow." Needless to say, the roses didn't get pruned nor the tomatoes staked. Now I always take my bucket, which has my clippers, scissors, hand rake, stakes, and twine in it. I'm prepared to take care of most garden woes on the spot, and my garden looks better as a consequence.

> Summer is a promissory note signed in June, its long days spent and gone before you know it, and due to be repeated next January.
>
> —Hal Borland

LOVELY LOBELIA

For years, I lived in a house on a steep hill that had no yard for gardening. But each year I would plant a variety of lobelia in a strawberry pot on my tiny landing. By summer, the pot would be covered in tiny, cascading blossoms—a meditation on the color blue: deep, almost midnight blue with a white center; solid royal blue, the palest baby blue, and bright violet blue. As evening fell, I would take my chair outside and watch the colors glow in the fading light.

> Sometimes in June, when I see unearned dividends of dew hung on every lupine, I have doubts about the real poverty of the sands.
>
> —Aldo Leopold

LEMON AID: HEALTHFUL LEMON CURD

We all know the adage, "when life gives you lemons," but we would update this classic with the suggestion to make lemon curd! With four ingredients, it is not a complex chore, but a delightful way to take your bounty of citrus and create a sweet and creamy joy-filled treat for you and your loved ones to enjoy for many months to come. What you'll need:

- 8 whole lemons (Meyer lemons are ideal, but any and all lemons will do)
- 2½ cups white sugar, granulated
- 2 cups fresh, unsalted butter
- 8 whole eggs, beaten

Have at the ready 8 clean glass jars you have sterilized in hot water. Half-pint Mason jars preferred.

Grate the zest of the lemons into a medium-sized saucepan. Squeeze juice from the lemons into a bowl—go for every drop! You should have around 1½ cups of juice. Add lemon juice to the saucepan, along with the sugar. Cut butter into small pieces and add to the pan, gradually.

Place your saucepan over low heat and stir until the butter has melted and the sugar dissolves. Strain the beaten eggs through a fine-mesh sieve into the pan with the lemon mixture. Cook on a medium heat for 10 to 15 minutes and stir frequently. As it heats up, the mixture will begin to thicken and take on a creamy consistency. When it coats the back of a spoon, you are well on your way to lemon curd!

When the lemon sauce is thick, remove the pan from the heat. Fill your hot sterilized jars with the lemon curd to within ⅛ inch of the rims. Wipe rims clean and top with hot lids. Screw bands onto the jars until finger tight. Process jars in a hot-water bath for ten minutes. Remove jars and stand them upright on a clean towel, away from drafts. Let jars sit undisturbed for 12 hours. Check for proper seals. Label the jars and store in a cool, dry place for up to a year.

Lemon Works for Everything

Instead of discarding lemon halves after you've used their juice for cooking or lemonade, save them to use as scrubbers for cleaning wood cutting boards without damaging them. You can also use fresh lemon juice mixed with baking soda to brighten white tiles, the sink or the tub, or make natural wood polish for floors by mixing a little fresh lemon juice with olive oil. This citrus fruit is a natural lightening agent that you can use in place of bleach, which should be used sparingly, if at all. Throw discolored white socks, towels, or shirts in a stockpot with water and a few used lemons; simmer for a little while to lighten. If you hang them outside to dry, the combination of sun and your low-cost lemon whitener will refresh your laundry until it is practically gleaming!

Easily clean cheese graters: cut the lemon in half and then run it over the grater. The acid in the lemon will help break down the fat in the cheese. If the food is really stuck on the grater, you can dip the lemon in table salt and the salt will serve as a scrubber; combined with the lemon, it will remove most foods.

Sanitize metal jewelry: The acid in lemon juice also works to remove tarnish. Use just a tablespoon of lemon juice concentrate to 1½ cups water. You can also dip your silver into lemon soda, and it will come out sparkling. But don't use this combo on gold or pearls.

Preserve meat and clean your cutting board: Lemon juice creates an acidic environment and bacteria need an alkaline environment to survive, so adding lemon to meat, produce, and even water inhibits bacterial growth. A handy antibacterial and natural way to clean your cutting board after cooking meat is to rub lemon juice on it and let sit overnight; rinse in the morning. The lemon juice will kill bacteria and leave your cutting board smelling fresh.

Naturally restore furniture: Mix equal parts mayonnaise, olive oil, and lemon juice together. When rubbed into wood furniture, this mixture will add oil to the wood, and the lemon juice will work to cut through any polish buildup on the furniture.

Prevent sticky rice: Add a teaspoon of lemon juice to the pot while the water's boiling to keep grains from sticking together. Lemon does prevent sticky rice, as do other citrus fruit lines, which help separate grains of rice and enhance the whiteness of the rice itself.

Get rid of grease: Copper pots are cleaned quickly with a lemon half dipped in salt. Rub over a tarnished copper-bottomed pot and you'll see magic; the same combo works great for removing grease from a cook top and from stainless steel pots and pans, too. If you have a real buildup of grease, use the lemon juice or half-lemon with coarse sea salt.

You turn to this citrus to enhance your water, but did you know it can also help perk up limp lettuce and kill weeds? The versatility of this beloved yellow fruit is fantastic.

Kill weeds: Forget chemical weed killers, which can be just as bad for you as they are for the planet. Control weeds with my lemon and white vinegar recipe, which is four parts lemon juice to one part white vinegar. Pour into a spray bottle, give it a shake, and head out to the garden.

GHOST GARDEN

Where I come from, there are many ramshackle houses. In shades of ghostly gray, their inhabitants have grown up and moved out, leaving the sad, spectral houses behind. The luckier of these houses, along the banks of the Ohio River, get reclaimed and become showplaces, at least one of which has graced the pages of Architectural Digest. Mostly, though, they wait. While the houses sag and creak, the gardens go wild! Plantings and hedges, once neat and tidy, are out of control, buzzing with birds, bees, and heaven knows what. Every spring and summer as a child, I would pick flowers in these abandoned yards and set up a table at the bottom of my driveway, to sell bouquets in old coffee cans to passing neighbors.

One such house I know burned to the ground during the night, leaving a charred and barren lot where once had been some river captain's pride. I was sad, because the hydrangeas were gone, and I had an eye on them, both for bouquets and for transplanting in my mother's garden. The next year, an amazing thing happened around the outer perimeters of the burned-down old manse: A "ghost garden" was growing in exactly the same formation! Bulbs, hedges, and even the hydrangeas all came back at an astonishing pace. And thanks to all the rusting copper pipes, hinges, and nails scattered half-buried in the soil after the fire, the hydrangeas, a pristine white the year before, were the bluest of blues. I decided not to take any. Those hydrangeas had been so loyal to that yard, they simply could not move anywhere else.

> Won't you come into my garden? I would like my roses to see you.
>
> **—Richard Sheridan**

WITH FAMILY AND FRIENDS

> Flowers leave some of their fragrance in the hand that bestows them.
>
> **—Chinese proverb**

FAIRY BOUQUETS

My dad was a great gardener and, when I was a little girl, he used to take me out early in the summer morning, before my mother woke up, to make fairy bouquets. We would pick only the tiniest flowers—violets, miniature roses, baby nasturtiums—place them into tiny bud vases or old spice jars, sometimes adding a bit of ribbon around the neck of the container, and put them at our breakfast plate. I loved doing it, and it was so much fun to see my mother's face when she came down to eat!

> Oh, this is the joy of the rose.
> That it blows,
> and goes
>
> —Willa Cather

MOON RIVER VINES

Growing up in the South, my summers were filled with shade trees, brazenly colored flowers, and choking vegetation in the form of wild morning glories and patches of kudzu that resembled small green seas. With so much growing and tangling about you, it's easy to understand why my family and I love gardening so much. My Uncle Robert loved vines and cultivated, cataloged, and saved seeds, which he doled out to the rest of us. His prize was blue moon river vine, whose rather ordinary-looking seeds held within their brown casing nothing short of a miracle to my cousins and me. Early each summer, Uncle Robert would take the seeds out of an old pill bottle and give each of us three to five of them, with instructions to plant them under a trellis or a porch column and keep them watered. Within six weeks, there would be a delicate vine with papery thin leaves that grew up at an astonishing rate. By mid-July the buds would appear, luminous white, like twisted-up tissue paper.

From then on, every summer night at dusk, we'd gather on the porch with our iced tea and try to act blasé as we furtively glanced every few minutes at the buds of the vine. Our childish patience would eventually be rewarded with a small sway from the vine, sometimes a tiny twitch, then ever so slowly, a bud would begin to open before very eyes, eventually, over the course of about half an hour, unfurling into a saucer-sized pure white flower. The smell was heavenly—rivaling that of magnolias and jasmine—but fainter and more elusive. We were never allowed to touch the flowers or—God forbid—pick them, and I honestly don't think I ever wanted to. I was awestruck by their amazing aliveness. Sometimes we'd turn off the porch light and get to stay up a little later than usual to see if a luna moth would visit the irresistible flowers; sometimes even a tiny bat would appear. Beyond the porch, the lightning bugs would signal to one another, and the symphony of night sounds serenaded us. It was magic.

> Fame is the scentless sunflower, with a gaudy crown of gold,
> But friendship is the breathing rose, with sweets in every fold.
>
> —Oliver Wendell Holmes

PERSONALIZED PUMPKINS

If you grow pumpkins, you can scratch names, dates, phrases, hearts, etc., into them with an ice pick or other sharp implement as they begin to grow. The scratch will heal over, and as your pumpkin gets bigger, so does your message. (Just think of the possibilities—kids especially enjoy such a surprise.)

DRAGON-LADY DAHLIAS

My aunt had a small house, where she cultivated one of the most envied gardens in northern Alabama. Her lawn was quilted with daffodils and tulips in the spring, and in summer she grew legions of leggy sunflowers and brilliant cannas. My favorites were her dahlias. They grew taller than me, and some of the flowers were bigger than my head. She would pick me a bouquet and we'd pretend that they were elegant, feathery hats as I held them behind my ears. They came in all shades, from lipstick pink to bright yellow, but there was one shade of red so intense it seemed to smolder. My aunt called these her dragon-lady dahlias. For me, they conjured up fantasy meetings with beautiful women dressed in exotic silk gowns or teddies with beaded headdresses, and long, tiny nails with crimson polish. They were intoxicating to look at, and I could spend hours engaged in my own little dramas among their searing faces. I buy dahlia bouquets every chance I get but have yet to find any as alluring as Aunt Myrtle's dragon-ladies.

GARDENER'S TEA

As you now know, tilling the back forty, harvesting your herbs and veggies, and weeding is a huge amount of work. It is one of life's greatest joys, without doubt, but nevertheless, many a sore back or set of aching knees have come as the result of a thriving garden. All the more reason for a tea that revives, refreshes, and offers relief to aching joints. From your store of dried herbs, gather these:

- 2 parts echinacea
- 2 parts chamomile
- 1 part mint
- 1 part anise seed
- 1 part thyme

A nice hot cup of this remedy will have you jumping back into the garden to plant more of all the herbs.

HOMEGROWN IS BEST

Quite often, almost as an afterthought as I am on my way out the door, I bring a small bouquet of seasonal flowers to a friend. What is in season is humble and hardly comparable to the thing a florist would deliver to your door. But the fragrance of fresh-cut sweet peas or the unexpected loveliness of onion tops and heliotrope mixed in with a few puny dahlias and zinnias make for a delightful surprise gift that is as wonderful to give as it is to receive.

> And what is so rare as a day in June?
> Then, if ever, come perfect days;
> Then Heaven tries the earth if it be in tune,
> And over it softly her warm ear lays.
>
> —James Russell Lowell

SPEAK THE LANGUAGE OF FLOWERS

We all know roses mean "I love you," but do you know the nonverbal messages of other flowers? The Victorians used to practice the "language of flowers" in which they would send little nosegays of homegrown flowers that were actually nonverbal poems. A bouquet of coreopsis and ivy, for example, would mean "always cheerful friendship." Such floral messages are called tussy-mussies, a term that dates back to the 1400s when those nosegays first came into fashion; they were routinely carried by both men and women.

The language of flowers was quite complex. If, for example, the flowers were presented upside down, the message was the opposite—an upside-down rose, for example, meant "I don't love you." If the bow or the flower bent to the left, the message referred to the receiver ("You have beautiful eyes"). If it bends to the right, the message refers to the sender. "I send loving thoughts" says the right-leaning pansy. If you added leaves to your tussy-mussy, they signaled hope, while thorns meant danger. When you received a tussy-mussy, touching it to your lips meant you agreed with the message's sentiments. If you tore off the petals and threw them down, you were sending a strong rejection of the sentiment.

Tussy-mussies are easy to make. Simply decide on your message and pick the appropriate flowers, leaving six inches of stem. Strip stems of leaves, and pick the largest flower for the center. Wrap its stem with floral tape. Then add the remaining flowers in a circle, taping the stems together as you go, keeping the height even, until you reach a diameter of about five inches. Then add greens, if any. Finish off by winding tape down the length of the stems, and add a ribbon streamer or a piece of lace as a bow. Viola! Send with a card explaining the flowers' meanings. Tussy-mussies should be kept in water.

Say It with Flowers

- **Apple blossom**: Preference
- **Azalea**: First love
- **Coreopsis**: Always cheerful
- **Cornflowers**: Healing, felicity
- **Daffodil**: Regard
- **Red dianthus**: Lively and pure affection
- **Heliotrope**: Accommodating disposition
- **Ivy**: Friendship
- **Johnny jump-up**: Happy thoughts
- **Lamb's ear**: Gentleness
- **Lavender**: Devotion
- **Lily of the Valley**: Return of happiness
- **Love-in-a-mist**: Kiss me twice before I rise
- **Mint**: Warmth of feeling
- **Oregano**: Joy
- **Pansy**: Loving thoughts
- **Red salvia**: Energy and esteem
- **Rosemary**: Devotion
- **Scented geranium**: Preference
- **Thyme**: Courage and strength
- **Violets**: Faithfulness
- **Wallflower**: Fidelity in adversity
- **White clover**: Good luck
- **Yarrow**: Health
- **Zinnia**: Thoughts of absent friends

A TIARA OF FIREFLIES

Our grandma always wore hairnets to keep her silver hair in place. As the nets wore out or snagged, Gram would give them to us girls. On special evenings, my sis and I would weave garlands of daisies and wildflowers and pin them in our hair. Our brother would bring in a canning jar full of fireflies, and we would tip that into Gram's hairnets, loosely fit them over our fancy hairdos, and have twinkling tiaras for an evening of garden play.

> The sound of birds stops the noise in my mind.
>
> **—Carly Simon**

SUSTAINING DELIGHTS

My favorite garden memories are from vegetable gardens my grandfather grew during the Depression, when I was a little girl. My father was a high school teacher long before unions and pay raises, and my grandparents had lost all their savings when the banks folded.

We spent all summer with my grandparents in Kentucky. My grandfather planted a garden large enough to feed all six of us and supply my mother and grandmother with produce to can for the winter. The garden was beautifully kept, with the lowest vegetables in the front—carrots, radishes, beets, parsnips. Then three kinds of beans—green and shell. Then pole beans, corn, and popcorn. Off to the side was a rambling mass of cucumbers and squash. Pumpkins were planted in between the last two rows of corn.

Every day, the noon meal consisted of any and all vegetables that were ready. And I always rode home at the end of the summer in the backseat of the car, squeezed in between boxes of full canning jars.

> It is forbidden to live in a town which has no greenery.
>
> **—The Jerusalem Talm**

INTO THE KITCHEN

> The smell of manure, of sun on foliage, of evaporating water, rose to my head; two steps further and I could look down into the vegetable garden enclosed within its tall pale fence of reeds—rich chocolate earth studded

> emerald green, frothed with the white of cauliflowers, jeweled with the purple globes of eggplant, and the scarlet wealth of tomatoes.
>
> —Doris Lessing

Summer's Healthful Harvest

We know gardening is good exercise, but research is now showing that eating the bounty from our gardens is also good for our health. Here's the lowdown on the most popular summer crops:

Tomatoes: One medium tomato has half the recommended daily allowance (RDA) of vitamin C and 20 percent of the RDA of fiber and vitamin A. It also contains lycopene, an antioxidant that appears to reduce the risk of heart attack and various cancers, including breast and prostate.

Corn: Excellent source of fiber and antioxidants—lutein and zeaxanthin that may lower the risk of macular degeneration, which is the leading cause of blindness in older folks.

Sweet Peppers: These are little powerhouses of vitamins A and C. Green peppers have twice as much vitamin C as oranges; yellow and red peppers have four times the C! They also are good sources of immune-system-enhancing B-6 and folic acid, which helps against heart disease and has been found to prevent neural tube defects in developing fetuses.

Zucchini: You may get sick of eating it, but this low-cal wonder is full of vitamins C and A and is also high in fiber, which helps prevent heart attacks and colon cancer.

> The work of a garden bears visible fruit—in a world where most of our labors seem suspiciously meaningless.
>
> —Pam Brown

THE SEASON OF PLENTY

No gardener worth his or her salt would be without a plethora of recipes to handle the abundance of green beans, corn, tomatoes, cucumbers, and especially zucchini that even a tiny garden can produce. Here are a few particularly tasty ones.

Stuffed Garden

This is a traditional recipe in Spain. You can make it with all one vegetable, but then you'll have to call it something else.

- 2 large onions, peeled but left whole
- 2 large whole green peppers
- 2 medium zucchinis
- pinch of saffron
- 2 bay leaves
- ¼ tsp. nutmeg
- 2 cloves
- 2 large fresh tomatoes
- 2 cloves garlic, peeled and chopped
- 14-oz. can chopped tomatoes
- 4 tablespoons olive oil
- salt and pepper
- 4 ounces bacon, trimmed of fat
- 2 tablespoons lightly toasted pine nuts
- 3 tablespoons bread crumbs
- 1 cup cooked rice
- 4 tbsp. grated Parmesan cheese
- 2 tbsp. white wine or water

Blanch the whole onions, peppers, and zucchini in a large pan of boiling water, removing peppers and zucchini after 5 minutes and onions after 15 minutes. Allow to cool. Pour off all but ½ cup of the water and add the saffron, bay leaves, nutmeg, and cloves and simmer for 10 minutes. Set spiced water aside.

Meanwhile, using a sharp knife and spoon, cut the tops of the tomatoes and scoop out the insides, leaving a shell thick enough for stuffing. Chop the tomato insides. In a small saucepan, combine 1 tablespoon oil, the garlic, and all the chopped tomatoes. Cook over medium heat for 10 minutes, until it becomes sauce-like. Add salt and pepper and set aside.

Preheat oven to 400° F. Using a spoon and a sharp knife, scoop out the centers of the onions, leaving a thin outer shell. Chop the centers. Cut the zucchini in half and scoop out the centers, and again, chop the insides. Cut the tops off the peppers and remove the seeds and inner membranes, keeping the peppers whole.

Heat the rest of the oil and the bacon, and sauté the chopped onions and zucchini until onion is wilted and bacon is crispy.

In a large bowl, combine the bacon mixture with the pine nuts, 2 tablespoons bread crumbs, half of the tomato sauce, salt and pepper, rice, and wine or water. Place the vegetable shells in a large baking pan and stuff with the stuffing mixture. Top with the remaining tomato sauce, bread crumbs, and grated cheese. Carefully pour the spiced water into the pan so that vegetables are sitting in about ½ inch of water. Bake until vegetable shells are soft to the touch and stuffing is heated through, about 35 minutes. During baking time, check baking pan and, if necessary, add more spiced water to keep vegetables from scorching.

Serves eight as a side dish, four as a main course.

Green Bean, Corn, and Tomato Salad

- 1 pound green beans cut into 1-inch lengths
- kernels from 3 ears of corn
- ½ cup white wine vinegar
- 6 tablespoons olive oil
- 5 tablespoons sugar
- 3 large tomatoes, chopped
- ½ cup chopped red onion
- ½ cup chopped fresh parsley
- salt and pepper to taste

Cook beans in large saucepan of boiling water for 2 minutes. Add corn kernels and cook until vegetables are crisp-tender about another 2 minutes. Drain well.

Whisk vinegar, oil, and sugar in a large bowl to blend. Add beans, corn, tomatoes, onion, and parsley. Toss to coat, season with salt and pepper. Cover and chill for at least 2 hours or overnight. Serves six.

Roasted Tomato and Red Pepper Soup

- 2¼ pounds tomatoes, halved lengthwise
- 2 large red bell peppers, seeded and quartered
- 1 onion, cut into thick slices
- 4 large garlic cloves, peeled
- 2 tablespoons olive oil
- 1 teaspoon (tsp) fresh thyme leaves, or ½ tsp dried
- water

Preheat oven to 450° F. Arrange tomatoes (cut side up), bell peppers, onion, and garlic cloves on a large baking sheet. Drizzle oil over, sprinkle generously with salt and pepper. Roast vegetables until browned and tender, turning peppers and onions occasionally, about 40 minutes. Remove from oven. Cool.

Transfer vegetables and any accumulated juices to food processor and add thyme. Puree soup, gradually adding 2 cups water to thin soup to desired consistency. Chill until cold, about 3 hours. (Can be prepared 1 day ahead. Cover and keep refrigerated. If soup becomes too thick, thin with water to desired consistency). Serves four.

Vegetable Gratin

- 2½ tablespoons butter
- 2 tablespoons olive oil
- 1 medium onion, chopped
- 2 garlic cloves, minced
- 1 medium-size green bell pepper, diced
- 8 smallish summer squashes (such as crookneck, pattypan, ronde de Nice, or zucchini), about 2 pounds total, cut into ½ inch cubes
- kernels from 2 ears corn
- salt and pepper to taste
- ¼ cup flour
- ½ cup cornmeal
- 4 tablespoons fresh basil or thyme, or combination of both
- 2 eggs, beaten
- 1 cup low-fat milk
- 3 tablespoons freshly grated Parmesan cheese

Preheat oven to 350°. Grease a shallow gratin dish or other baking dish with ½ tablespoon of the butter. Place 1 tablespoon butter and the olive oil in a skillet over medium heat. Add the onions, garlic, and green pepper: sauté over medium-high heat for 5 minutes.

Add the squash, corn, and salt and pepper, and sauté another 4 to 5 minutes, until the squash in nearly tender. Remove from heat, and set aside.

Mix together the flour, cornmeal, basil and/or thyme. Stir in the eggs, milk, and vegetables.

Spoon the mixture into the prepared dish and bake for 25 to 30 minutes or until a crust has formed and a knife inserted in the center comes out nearly clean. Dot with the remaining 1 tablespoon butter, sprinkle the cheese on top, and bake for 7 to 10 minutes longer, until the crust has browned slightly and the edges are bubbling and crispy. Serve hot or at room temperature. Serves six.

Caprese Salad

This delight only works with vine-ripened tomatoes. If all you have are the rubbery store versions, wait until you can find some real tomatoes.

- 1 tablespoon fresh lemon juice
- 6 tablespoons olive oil
- 3 tablespoons red wine vinegar
- 4–5 tomatoes, cut into ½-inch slices
- 1 large red onion, julienned
- 8 ounces mozzarella, thinly sliced
- 15–20 fresh basil leaves

Combine lemon juice, olive oil, and vinegar in a jar or container with an airtight lid. Shake vigorously for a full minute. Chill.

On a large plate, layer onion slices, tomatoes, and mozzarella. Garnish liberally with fresh basil. Pour the dressing over the salad immediately before serving.

Serves six to eight as an appetizer.

Old-Fashioned Mustard Pickles

This recipe from my French grandmother is not for the faint of heart. It makes the puckery-est pickles I've ever tasted. Everyone in my family loves them—and I hope you will too. It makes a lot, but you can cut the recipe down proportionally.

- 4 dry quarts small pickling cucumbers, with stems (a dry quart is 1/6 more than a liquid quart, says Joy of Cooking)
- ½ gallon white vinegar
- ½ cup salt
- ½ cup dry mustard
- 1 teaspoon powdered alum

Wash cucumbers carefully. In a large crock, mix remaining ingredients and add cucumbers (add more vinegar if necessary to cover cucumbers completely in liquid). Cover and store in a cool, dark place for three weeks, stirring occasionally. When pickles are ready, refrigerate for longer life. Makes 1 crock. (If you have no crock, mix the ingredients in a large bowl, place cucumbers in jars, then pour vinegar mixture over. Store in cool dark place for three weeks, shaking jars occasionally.)

Crisp Delight

One of my greatest garden pleasures is to receive compliments on the rhubarb-strawberry crisp I bake for almost every summer barbeque. Our rhubarb plant was well established in the garden when we moved into our house fifteen years ago. The plant is so prolific that I give away a fresh bunch to every rhubarb lover who enters the door. Though not all our guests favor this beautiful celery-like plant topped with magnificent poisonous leaves, when they see the crisp warm from the oven with its sugary top and juicy bottom, they cannot resist this old standby. Add ice cream and wait for compliments to come pouring in.

- 3 cups rhubarb, sliced
- 2 cups strawberries, whole or sliced
- juice of 1 lemon
- 1 stick butter, softened
- 1 cup granulated sugar
- 1 cup flour

Preheat oven to 400°F. Combine rhubarb, strawberries, and lemon juice in a 9 x 13-inch baking pan. In a medium bowl, combine the butter, sugar, and flour until crumbly and then spread over rhubarb mixture. Bake uncovered for 20 minutes or until crisp is bubbly and top browned. Serves six.

Plenty of Pesto

No book of garden how-to's would be complete without a pesto recipe. Pesto is usually made with basil (a prolific grower), but can also be made with cilantro or parsley, or a combination. All you need is a large quantity of fresh herbs. Pesto can be frozen and lasts for several months in the freezer. If your basil is going to seed, make a large batch of pesto, minus the cheese, and freeze it.

- ½ cup olive oil
- 1 clove garlic
- 1 tablespoon pine nuts
- ¼ teaspoon salt
- ½ cup grated Parmesan cheese
- 4 cups basil, cilantro, or parsley, washed

Place all ingredients, except the basil, in a food processor. Process until smooth. Add the basil a little at a time, until pesto is smooth. Makes 1 cup.

> The best things that come out of the garden are gifts for other people.
>
> —Jamie Jobb

THE FRUITS OF SUMMER

I love summer fruit—especially plums, nectarines, and cherries. I think one of the reasons they taste so delicious is because their season is so short. I never quite manage to get my fill, and then they're gone from the stores. Once, I went cherry-picking in upstate New York, and even with my "one for the bucket—one for my mouth" picking method, I never did reach the saturation point.

When I was a teenager, I taught swimming at an overnight camp on a lake in my hometown. Even though it was so close to home, I lived at camp, and while I greatly enjoyed that first taste of freedom, the food—instant mashed potatoes and powdered eggs—left much to be desired. So every few days, as I was standing on the docks supervising the swimmers, my father would drive up in his VW bug and hand a paper sack out the window: my fresh-fruit supply.

Stuffed Baked Peaches

- 10 fresh peaches, pitted and halved
- 1 egg yolk
- 7 tablespoons butter, softened
- 1 cup crushed Amaretto di Saronno cookies

Remove one spoonful of peach flesh from each peach, puree, and set aside. Cream 6 tablespoons of butter in a bowl, stirring in egg yolk, peach puree, and crushed cookies until well combined. Fill each peach half with a generously rounded scoop of the mixture.

Place the peach halves, open side up, in a large glass casserole with the remaining tablespoon of butter, and bake in a preheated oven at 375° for 5–7 minutes, or until cookie mixture is lightly browned. Serve peaches at room temperature with crème fraiche or ice cream. Serves ten.

Peach or Nectarine Clafouti

This is a marvelous low-fat dessert that's perfect for late summer, when peaches and nectarines are abundant.

- 1¼ cups low-fat milk
- ¼ cup granulated sugar
- 3 eggs
- 1 tablespoon vanilla extract
- ⅛ teaspoon salt
- ⅔ cup all-purpose flour, sifted
- 1½ pounds peaches or nectarines, peeled, pitted, and sliced
- 1 tablespoon powdered sugar

Preheat oven to 350°F. Grease a medium-sized baking dish.

Combine the milk, granulated sugar, eggs, vanilla, salt, and flour in a mixing bowl; beat with an electric mixer until the mixture is frothy, about 3 minutes.

Pour enough of the batter into the prepared baking dish to make a ¼-inch-deep layer. Bake for 2 minutes. Remove the dish from the oven. Spread the fruit in a layer over the cooked batter and pour the remaining batter on top.

Bake until the clafouti is puffed and browned and a knife inserted in the center comes out clean, about 30 to 35 minutes. Sprinkle with powdered sugar just before serving. Serves six.

Lemon Tea Bread

Here's a summer treat for those who grow lemon balm.

- 1 tablespoon finely chopped lemon balm
- 1 tablespoon finely chopped lemon thyme
- ¼ cup low-fat milk
- 2 cups flour
- ¼ teaspoon salt
- 1½ teaspoons baking powder
- 6 tablespoons butter, softened
- 1 cup sugar
- 2 eggs, beaten
- 1 tablespoon grated lemon zest
- juice of 2 lemons
- confectioners' sugar, about ¼–½ cup

Preheat the oven to 325°. Grease a 9 x 5 x 3-inch loaf pan.

In a small saucepan, gently heat the milk with the lemon balm and thyme until just before it boils. Remove from heat and let steep until cool.

Combine the flour, salt, and baking powder in a medium bowl. In a large bowl, cream the butter and sugar together until fluffy. Add the eggs, one at a time, and beat well. Add the lemon zest, then part of the flour mixture, then some of the milk. Beat well and continue alternating until well combined.

Pour into prepared pan and bake for about 1 hour or until a toothpick inserted into the center comes out clean. While loaf is cooking, place lemon juice in a small bowl with enough confectioners' sugar to make a thick but still pourable glaze. Stir well.

Remove bread from pan and place on a wire rack that has been set over waxed paper. Pour glaze over top and allow to cool.

Makes 1 loaf.

> Happiness depends, as Nature shows,
> less on exterior things than most suppose.
>
> —**William Cowper**

EDIBLE BLOSSOMS

Yes, many flowers (minus stems and leaves) are quite wonderful-tasting, but before you start randomly eating flowers from your garden, be sure you know what you are doing—some are deadly poisonous. And of course, if you use pesticides or herbicides in your garden, do not eat unwashed blooms. These caveats aside, flowers do wonderfully in salads, as garnishes for serving platters, and to decorate cakes. The following is a list of some of the edible beauties.

- Bee balm
- Calendula
- Daylilies
- Hollyhocks
- Marigolds
- Nasturtiums

- Pansies
- Roses
- Scarlet runner bean
- Sunflowers
- Violets

Candied Flowers

These delectable treats are easy to create. Use them on top of ice cream or cakes. Pick the flowers fresh in the early morning.

- Violet blossoms
- 1 or 2 egg whites, depending on how many flowers you use
- Rose petals
- Superfine sugar, to taste

Gently wash flowers and dry with a clean towel. Beat the egg whites in a small bowl. Pour the sugar into another bowl. Carefully dip the flowers into the egg whites, then roll in sugar, being sure to cover all sides. Set flowers on a cookie sheet and allow to dry in a warm place. Store in a flat container with wax paper between layers. These will last for several days.

SATISFYING SIPS

You can make all kinds of delicious drinks from the garden.

Here are a few recipes to get you started.

Limeade with Rose Water and Peppermint Syrup

Peppermint Syrup:

- ¼ cup water
- 1¼ cups superfine sugar
- zest of 1 lemon
- ½ cup coarsely chopped fresh peppermint

Limeade:

- ½ cup lime juice
- 2 tablespoons rose water
- fresh peppermint sprigs for garnish

To make peppermint syrup, place the water and sugar in a medium saucepan. Bring to a boil, stirring to dissolve the sugar. Add the mint and lemon zest and remove from heat. Allow to cool with the lid on. Strain the mixture, discarding the mint and lemon zest. Makes 1½ cups syrup (refrigerate unused portion for future limeades).

To make limeade: Into each of 2 glasses, pour ¼ cup lime juice. Add 1 tablespoon rose water to each glass, stirring well. Add peppermint syrup to limeade to taste, and stir again. Fill glasses with crushed ice. Garnish with fresh peppermint sprigs before serving. Serves two.

Homemade Ginger Ale

This is very simple to make, but you've got to drink it up after you make it—the carbonation won't last long, and it shouldn't be sealed, or else there could be an explosion.

- 3 tablespoons ginger root, peeled
- 4 quarts boiling water
- 1 lime
- 3 cups sugar
- 3 tablespoons cream of tarter
- 1 tablespoon yeast

Pound the ginger until it's a mash. Pour the boiling water over it, and add the lime, sugar, and cream of tartar. Cover with a cloth and let cool to lukewarm. Add yeast, let rest for 6 hours. Chill, strain, and serve. Makes 4 quarts.

Unfermented Ginger Ale

This one has no carbonation and can be made in a matter of minutes.

- 4 ounces ginger root
- 4 lemons
- 2 quarts boiling water
- 2 cups lemon juice
- sugar and water to taste
- mint leaves, optional

Finely chop the ginger and lemons. Pour the boiling water over and steep 5 minutes. Strain out and discard the solids. Chill the liquid. Add lemon juice and sugar to taste, dilute with water if necessary. Serve over ice with mint leaves, if desired.

Makes 2 quarts.

Iced Delights

Spice up your ice by adding fruit, herbs, and edible flowers to the ice trays after you've filled them and before freezing. They taste great and add a visual kick to a festive occasion. Here are some fun alternatives to plain old H2O.

- Sprigs of rosemary, dill, lemongrass, or mint
- Roses, carnations, nasturtiums, lavender, or pansies
- Raspberries, blueberries, cucumber, lemon, or lime zest

PRESERVING THE BOUNTY

With the invention of the freezer, folks no longer had to can their vegetables from the garden and were able to better preserve both texture and flavor. I remember my mother, in the hot days of August, starting in the early morning to blanch the zucchini and beans from the garden to freeze for the winter. Now it turns out that many vegetables don't even need to be blanched before freezing. With peas, string beans, cabbage, zucchini, celery, broccoli, onions, and green peppers, you can just clean and cut to size. Place in plastic containers with lids, cover with water, and freeze. When completely frozen, remove the block of vegetables from the container, place in a freezer bag and return to the freezer. The downside is that vegetables won't keep as long this way (between three and five months), but if you are not freezing a tremendous amount, it should work just fine.

OLD ROSES

Perhaps because of the advantage of coming from a family of flower lovers, I am a bit of a snob about roses. For me, they have to be old, old, old, or I turn up my nose. You can tell the difference between old roses and the new fancy hybrid kinds so easily—the distinctive scents, the big falling-apart, the loose petals. Old roses are like the women that grew them originally, like my aunts—very dignified, wearing simple and subtle colors, and with a scent of purest essence of rose. New roses are exotic and pretty to look at, but it is the old roses that have rooted in my memory and stay forever.

> If I give you a rose, you will not doubt of God.
>
> —Clement of Alexander

Rose Wine

Here's an old-fashioned treat. Don't do this if you spray your roses with insecticide. (Which we don't advocate, anyway.) Be sure to thoroughly clean the roses, and do not store wine in metal containers or stir with metal utensils—metal reacts to the acid in wine.

- 2 oranges
- 3 quarts washed and lightly packed rose petals
- 1 gallon boiling water
- 3 pounds sugar
- 1 package yeast
- 5 white peppercorns

Rind the oranges and set oranges aside. Cut up rind. Place the rose petals in a large saucepan. Pour the boiling water in and add the orange rind and sugar. Boil for 20 minutes, remove from heat, and cool. Add the yeast, dissolved in warm water per package instructions, the juice from the oranges, and the peppercorns. Pour into stoneware crock, cover and let sit where temperature is between 60 and 80°F for two weeks. Strain, discard petals, rinds, and peppercorns, and bottle in sterilized jars, corking lightly for about 3 months or until the rind has completed fermenting. To store wine, seal bottles with paraffin. Makes about 1 gallon.

> Innumerable as the stars of night, or stars of morning,
> dewdrops which the sun impearls on every leaf and every flower
>
> —Milton

BEAUTIFYING YOUR HOME

> To pick a flower is so much more satisfying than just observing it or photographing it… So in later years, I have grown in my garden as many flowers as possible for children to pick.
>
> —Anne Scott-James
>
> O the green things growing the green things growing,
> the fair sweet smell of the green things growing.
>
> —Dinah Mulock Craik

Pebbles for Your Thoughts

Instead of buying gravel or garden rocks, consider collecting what you need from beaches, mountains, riverbeds, etc. Each hand-selected rock will mean more—and be more beautiful—than a pile of uniform stones. Feel free to paint or decorate them too!

> Show me your garden, provided it be your own,
> and I will tell you what you are like.
>
> —Alfred Austin
>
> There is no gardening without humility. Nature is constantly sending even its oldest scholars to the bottom of the class for egregious blunder.
>
> —Alfred Austen

Window Box Basics

The key to colorful window boxes is choosing the right combination of plants. One really effective combination is a single type of flower in just one color: bright yellow begonias for example, or all red petunias. Or you can try a variety of blue flowers: pale and dark lobelias combined with *Anchusa capensis* is a wonderful combination. Or the tried-and-true pink geraniums with white petunias and variegated ivy. Think also about shapes (trailing combined with bushy and upright) and foliage (greens break up the arrangement and make it eye-catching). Consider where the box is located and choose plants appropriately. If it is in shade all day, be sure all the plants you choose are shade-loving. If one type of plant likes a lot of water and another doesn't, it would be best not to plant them together. Purchase enough plants so they can be tightly packed into the box. This will give a lush display when they flower.

To make a window box, make sure there is adequate drainage from the container; if not, drill a couple of small holes. Add a layer of broken terra-cotta pieces and then fill with dirt halfway. Experiment with placement while plants are still in original containers: tall, upright flowers in the back, trailing ones at front and sides. When you have a pleasing arrangement, water plants thoroughly, then remove from pots, fill box with dirt to ¾ inch below the rim, and add the plants. Water thoroughly and add soil if necessary.

Be sure to water frequently, even once or twice a day during the hottest weather, and feed with a liquid plant food once a week. If frequent watering is difficult for you, consider buying a window box with a water reservoir. To keep your box looking lovely, pinch back young plants and prune leggy stems. Deadheading will help plants produce more flowers.

Enchanted Cottage Non-Toxic Flour Paint

In case you want to paint your window boxes or fence, or even walls or a flower pot, here is a safe and non-toxic way to make your own paint. Most of us don't even realize that these "store-bought" corporate paints, varnishes, and latexes are off-gassing and are bad for our lungs, brain, skin, and everything else. There are so many toxins around us that reducing this in our personal environment is essential. Gather the following:

- 2 cups wheat flour
- 6 cups cold water
- ⅔ cup mica filler (available at any art or craft store)
- 3 cups boiling water
- 1 cup screened clay (easily found at any art or craft shop)
- Natural dye of your choice

Whisk the flour into a bowl with 3 cups of cold water; add the flour mixture into 3 cups boiling water and cook at a simmer for ten minutes. Mix very well. Now remove from the heat and add in the remaining 3 cups of cold water. Let cool while you mix the mica and clay together thoroughly, in a separate bowl, and fold into the flour paste. Feel free to add natural coloring agents such as tea, turmeric, berry juice, wine, or whatever color you are needing for your décor. Flour paint is especially useful as a substitute "whitewash" for outdoor walls, fences, and sheds. It usually requires more than one coat of paint. As you can tell from the ingredients, this has way less chemicals in it and is as natural as can be. Stop breathing in unnecessary toxins; grab a brush and start beautifying!

COLOR MAGIC

If you are going to paint your walls, fences, furniture and she-sheds, you should be very considered in your choice of color. Here is a simple guide to color magic for your explorations:

Red is for action, passion, vitality, strength, survival, fertility, courage, sexuality, conflict, independence, assertiveness, competition, and standing out.

Orange brings joy, creativity, expressiveness, intellect, releasing addiction, business success and ambition, vitality, fun, new ideas, and sharing good times with others.

Yellow is used for enjoyment, inspiration, success, happiness, learning, memory and concentration, persuasion, imagination, charm, confidence, and travel.

Green is great for prosperity, abundance, money, physical and emotional healing, growth, luck, marriage, plant magic, acceptance, and counteracting envy and possessiveness.

Light blue represents spirituality, tranquility, peace, protection, and growth.

Blue is used for communication, willpower, focus, forgiveness, good fortune, truth, patience, harmony at home, orderliness, removing bad vibrations, sincerity, and true-blue loyalty.

Indigo is ideal for spiritual guidance, mindfulness, psychic ability, divination, meditation, ambitions, dignity, and overcoming depression.

Violet is the color of spirituality, connection to higher self, insight, clarity, and the divine feminine.

Purple is for wisdom, cronehood and elders, influence, driving away evil, changing one's luck, independence, breaking habits, and spiritual power.

Lavender is the color to use for aspiration, knowledge, and accessing intuition.

Pink is the color of love, compassion, nurturing, femininity, friendship, romance, partnership, spiritual and emotional healing, protection of children, and personal inner work.

Brown is good for house blessings, animal magic, material goods, stability, food, and forests.

Gray is best for contemplation and removing negativity in your environment.

White connotes newness, cleansing, purity, peace, balance, healing, truth, and spirituality.

Black stands for grounding, wisdom, learning, protection and security, reversing hexes, removing negative energy, transforming, defense, scrying, and secrets.

Silver is used for feminine divinity, psychic awareness, intuition, dreams, victory, communication, luck, and moon magic.

Gold represents masculine divinity, great fortune, abundance, prosperity, understanding, divination, fast luck, positive attitude, justice, health, attraction, luxury, and magic involving the sun.

Copper brings business success, passion, money, fertility, and career growth.

Vacation Tips for Houseplants

- While you are away from home, you can make sure that your plants don't end up in the great compost pile in the sky by following these simple tips:
- Before you leave, pull your plants out of hot spots so they will not dry out so quickly, and move them to the coolest, darkest spots in your house. Bring any deck plants inside, again to the coolest, darkest locations.
- Do not leave plants in a bucket of water or deep saucer while you're gone. Too much water can rot the roots. Instead, fill trays or saucers with pebbles and water and group plants together to raise humidity; and remember, if the house is closed and lights are off, your plants will need less water.

If you're going to be gone for any length of time, be sure to have someone come in and water once a week.

> What continues to astonish me about a garden
> is that you can walk past it in a hurry,
> see something wrong, stop to set it right,
> and emerge an hour or two later breathless, contented,
> and wondering what on earth happened.
>
> —Dorothy Gilman

MY CUTTING GARDEN

One of the little things I take true delight in on a regular basis is flower arranging. I'm not good with my hands (my sister used to leave the house in fear when I was learning to sew in junior high), but I have the urge to make something beautiful, and over the years I have discovered that flower arranging is my creative medium. It takes no manual dexterity and, since I planted a cutting garden in my backyard (I can't stand the prices at the florist), no money either. I have an entire cabinet filled with containers (vases I have been given over the years, the beautiful blue bottle a certain type of mineral water comes in, an old jam jar) as well as things scavenged from store-bought bouquets (curly willow, pieces of floral foam, rocks I use to stabilize large arrangements). Every once in a while, I consider actually investing in this pastime of mine—buying some floral frogs, getting some vases of certain heights and widths (why, oh why, are the containers I have always too tall or too short or too wide?). But there is something about my low-tech, New England frugal approach that I enjoy, so I continue to make do.

I take great delight in the fact that any time of the year (okay, so I live in California), I can walk outside and find something blooming to liven up my bedroom, the kitchen table, or the shelf in the bathroom. I have never read a book about the principles of flower arranging, and I don't spend too much time on it—maybe five minutes at the most. For me, the joy comes from the ease with which it is possible to make something pleasing to look at: selecting an old yellow mustard jar, filling it with nasturtiums, and placing it on the kitchen table. Ongoing beauty meal after meal, in only two minutes!

> A garden is a private world, or it is nothing.
>
> —Eleanor Perenyi

LONG-LASTING BOUQUETS

When cutting flowers from the garden, there are a few tricks in gathering them that will ensure long life:

1. Be sure to cut them in the early morning or evening.
2. Whether using scissors or a sharp knife (there's disagreement over which is better), cut the stems at a deep angle when the buds are half-open (except for zinnias, marigolds, asters, and dahlias, which should be picked in full bloom).
3. Remove leaves at the bottoms of the stems (they rot) and plunge flowers immediately up to their necks in tepid water.
4. Let sit in a cool place for four to twelve hours before arranging.

Certain flowers require different treatment. Daffodils should be kept separate for twelve hours to dry up their sap which clogs the stems of other flowers. When using tulips or irises, be sure to remove the white portion of the stems—only the green part can absorb water. Dip stem ends of poppies and dahlias in boiling water before placing in tepid water to prevent them from oozing a substance that can clog the stems and cause the flowers to wilt.

PRETTY PAPER CUP LIGHTS

These are great strung on your front porch or out on a deck for a party. The trick is to poke enough of the design in the cup to let the light through, but not to cut it completely.

- Cut-out patterns
- Solid colored paper cups
- Pencil
- Craft knife
- Large craft pin (looks like the letter T) or large safety pin
- String of small indoor/outdoor Christmas lights

Find in a craft-pattern book or draw on your own, a small design that will fit on a paper cup (a small flower or a star works fine). Cut out the design to make a pattern. Hold the pattern against a cup you have turned upside down, and trace the pattern lightly onto the side. With the craft knife, cut along sections of the pencil marks and push the cup in a bit along the cut. Do not cut out the design! The little cuts along the pattern will let the light through. With the pin, poke holes along the top and bottom of the design for effect. Punch a hole in the bottom of each cup the size of the Christmas lights and push the bulb through. String up when finished.

> Every flower about a house certifies to the refinement of somebody. Every vine climbing and blossoming tells of love and joy.
>
> **—Robert Ingersoll**

THE ROMANCE OF LAVENDER

To me, there is little as wondrous as lavender. I grow at least three varieties at all times and love the shapes each have to offer, distinct yet so easy to know they are bound together as a family. As I wander in my lavender patch, I inhale the oily scent that sticks to my clothes and my fingers. I'm like a foreigner who returns to a café visited long ago, so long ago, he has forgotten its name. One has a small barrel-shaped flower that, when dried, I keep in a small lace pocket. A scented memory that keeps the memory close. Another has a long flower stem that rises up to greet the sky, both day and night. A single bloom to paint the air with its fragrance. The third has a long flower stem that splits into three or four flower bundles, a lamp post for bees searching for pollen. All have a scent redolent of foreign travel, of mystery and magic.

> Nor rural sights alone, but rural sounds, exhilarate the spirit, and restore the tone of languid nature.
>
> **—William Cowper**

Luscious Lavender

As a scent, lavender is enjoying huge popularity these days. Maybe because it is considered a romantic yet clean fragrance that is appealing to both men and women, unlike rose, for example, which is associated just with women. Used for centuries to calm nerves, you can enjoy the incomparable scent of lavender in your own home in many ways: bundles of dried lavender, lavender pillows and sachets, and lavender bath products. Lavender is said to be good for sore, tired feet. Simply add a few drops of essential oil to a basin and place feet in water. One incredibly easy thing to do is to buy lavender essential oil and scent your closet or chest of drawers by placing the oil on a cotton ball and rubbing it along the insides of wooden drawers and shelves. The wood will slowly release the fragrance.

Lavender Bouteille

This is a woven lavender wand (*bouteille* means bottle in French) used as a sachet to scent closets and underwear drawers. You can make an elaborate one that is woven like a basket, but I prefer the simplest possible.

- 40 long stalks of freshly cut lavender, picked at the height of bloom
- twine or raffia
- beautiful ribbon, optional

Gather the stalks together in one big bunch. Remove any side shoots and tie together tightly, just under the flowers, with twine or raffia. Bend down all the stalks evenly over the lavender blossoms and tie with twine again. Even off the ends with scissors. If you like, you can use a decorative ribbon at the end. To release the scent, simply squeeze the bouteille.

HEAVENLY HYDRANGEAS

Hydrangeas, those pink, blue, and white wonders, are hot these days, so popular that police in California are reporting that the blooms are being stolen from people's yards. (My hydrangea problem is of the four-legged variety: deer keep eating the buds before they open.) If you have some of your own, late summer, when the blossoms have just started to dry on the bush but before the color has faded, is the time to harvest for drying.

Getting perfect, colorful, full, fluffy dried heads isn't completely easy, however. Flower experts report only about a 50 percent success rate, so it's best to start out with a lot of flowers. Lace-cap hydrangeas are particularly difficult; try the mop-head variety instead. The trick is to remove all the leaves, and re-cut the stems as soon as you get into the house. Then hold the stems over a flame for 20 seconds, then submerge in cold water up to the flower head for 2 days. Pour off all but ½ inch of water and let the rest evaporate in a warm dry place, such as next to your water heater. When the water is gone, the blooms should be dry.

> Patience is a flower that grows not in everyone's garden.
>
> —English proverb

NOURISHING BODY AND SOUL

> Summer is the time when one sheds one's tensions with one's clothes, and the right kind of day is jeweled balm for the battered spirit. A few of those days and you can become drunk with the belief that all's right with the world.
>
> —Ada Louise Huxtable
>
> Earth and sky, wind and trees, rivers and fields, the mountains and the sea. All are excellent schoolmasters and teach some of us more than we could ever learn from books.
>
> —Anonymous

Get Your Glow Back with Scented Salts

This is fabulous for exfoliating dry skin, particularly when your tan is starting to flake. Be sure not to use on your face or neck; it's too rough for that.

- 2 cups sea salt
- 7 drops of your favorite essential oil
- 1 ounce sweet almond oil

Place salt and oils in a bowl and combine with your fingers. Stand or sit naked in an empty bathtub and rub salt mixture onto your skin with your hands, starting with your feet. Massage in a circular motion. As the salts fall, pick up and reuse until you reach your neck. Then fill the tub with warm water and soak.

Peaches and Cream Moisturizer

Blend together in a blender or food processor one peach and enough heavy cream to create a spreadable consistency. Massage onto your skin when needed. Refrigerate unused portion. (And use up within a day or so, or it will "turn.")

Herbal Facial Toner

This is a really easy, all-natural skin freshener, a perfect pick-me-up for hot, humid weather.

- 1½ cups witch hazel extract
- ½ cup rose water
- 1 tablespoon grated lime peel
- 1 tablespoon dried rosemary leaves
- 2 drops lavender oil
- 2 drops rosemary oil

Combine the witch hazel and rose water in a clean glass jar with a tight-fitting lid. Shake well to thoroughly combine. Add the remaining ingredients and again shake well, this time for 5 minutes. Store the jar a in a cool dark place, shaking five minutes a day for two weeks. At the end of that period, strain the mixture and store the remaining liquid in an airtight container, where it will last up to six weeks if refrigerated. For extra refreshment, try keeping a spritz bottle full of toner, and using it straight from the refrigerator.

Skin Soother Bath

This wonderful recipe will soothe any skin condition, from heat rash to chicken pox. It's wonderful for your skin and hair, so use it even when you're problem-free!

- ½ cup finely ground oatmeal
- 1 cup virgin olive oil
- 2 cups aloe vera gel
- 20 drops rosemary or lavender oil

Combining the ingredients in a large bowl, stir well. Add to a warm running bath.

Citrus Toner

- ¼ cup lemon peel, freshly grated
- ¼ cup grapefruit peel, freshly grated
- 1 cup mint leaves
- 1 cup water

Add mint and citrus peelings to rapidly boiling water. Continued to boil for 1 to 2 minutes or until peels become soft and slightly translucent. Remove from heat. Cool and strain. Store in refrigerator or freezer. This will last 2 to 3 weeks.

WEEDING THERAPY

When three things go wrong by midmorning, there's only one thing to do: head for the garden. The beans needed weeding. Great; something to work out my resentments on. I knelt and started; the lamb's-quarters and pigweed pulled out easily, so I ripped them out angrily, in big handfuls. That felt good. After a few minutes, I was enjoying the comforting feel of the soft, warm earth. I noticed the tiny beans were coming along just as they should, in elegant clusters hanging straight down. As the weed heap grew and the row of handsome, weed-free plants extended behind me, I realized I wasn't frowning anymore: actually, I was smiling. Is gardening therapeutic? You bet it is.

A HATFUL OF BEAUTY

For a summer garden party, beautify your old straw hat with a ribbon of fresh flowers. All you need besides the hat is raffia, scissors, and some flowers. Try flowers that will last a long time out of water—sunflowers, statice, yarrow, chrysanthemums, carnations, and daisies are best, as are sturdy greens like sword ferns. Cut the greens and flowers with long enough stems to bundle. Separate each kind and create hand-sized bunches of each. Set aside. Cut several strands of raffia long enough to not only go around the hat's crown, but also wrap around the flower bundles.

Knot the strands together at one end. Starting six inches from the knotted end, twist the raffia around the stems of one bunch of flowers several times. Lay the next bunch as far from the previous bunch as you like, and repeat the wrapping process. Continue down the length of raffia until you have a garland long enough to go around the hat.

Place the garland on the hat and tie the two ends of raffia together; tuck any loose raffia under the flowers. To keep fresh for several days, store hats in the refrigerator in a plastic bag.

> Simplicity is the essence of happiness.
>
> —**Cedric Bledsoe**

A WAKE-UP CALL

I was standing in our community garden, looking at the colossal collection of cantaloupe that I had grown—my first-ever attempt. Vistas of an alternative career opened—I would leave my career as a physician and become a champion cantaloupe farmer! (Little did I know this was one of life's "fabulous firsts." That day was over twenty years ago, and since that time I've not successfully grown even one more.)

As I stood relishing my achievement, out of the corner of my eye, I spotted a lovely teenage girl in a nearby plot. She was staking up some tomato plants. She was a patient of mine, a schizophrenic. She had her head cocked, listening intently. There was a relaxed smile on her face, and I realized that in this peaceful place, she was not hearing her usual voices of terror. She was listening to the whisper of the winds and the song of the birds. I left quietly.

NATURAL HEADACHE REMEDIES

Here are two ways to handle a headache with ingredients from the garden. The first is a Midwestern pioneer recipe; the second is an old-fashioned German cure.

Headache Pillow

- ½ ounce ground cloves
- 2 ounces dried lavender
- 2 ounces dried marjoram
- 2 ounces dried rose petals
- 2 ounces betony rose leaf
- 1 teaspoon orris root
- Two pieces of cotton batting, slightly smaller than a handkerchief
- 2 handkerchiefs
- Lace or ribbon, optional

Grind spices, flowers, and orris root together, either by hand with a mortar and pestle or in the food processor. Pack the powder in between the two pieces of cotton. Sew together three sides of the two handkerchiefs. Place the cotton "pillow" inside and hand-sew the fourth side tight enough that the contents don't leak out. Decorate with lace or ribbons, if desired. To use, lie on pillow and inhale fragrance or place over eyes.

> As an instrument of planetary home repair, it is hard to imagine anything as safe as a tree.
>
> —Jonathan Weiner

Rosy Headache Remedy

- 1 quart white rose petals
- 1 quart jar, sterilized
- About 1 quart 90-proof vodka or rubbing alcohol

Pack the jar with the rose petals. Pour the vodka over and let stand, covered, for at least 24 hours. Rub on forehead, temples, and back of neck.

WATER WISDOM

Every year the sitting area on my deck shrinks as I buy more pots and fill them with summer flowers. I water them slowly, pot by pot. Once in a while, I try to do two things at once—water and talk on the phone. But it's distracting to pay attention to the person at the other end while I'm watching the water flow into the rich brown soil and smiling at the flowers. So, by the beginning of July, I just let the phone ring when I'm watering.

As each plant soaks up the wet nourishment, I stand amid the air, the smells, and the sounds of life, and all of them help to slow my world down, quiet my thoughts, and give me time to pause.

Feng Shui Your Garden with a Fountain

For an almost instant homemade fountain, insert an inexpensive electric pump into a large ceramic planter, then fill it with water and plug it in. Place your creation in a bed of low, flowering ground cover to highlight your landscaping, or install it on the deck or patio and relax to the soothing sound of flowing water.

CHAPTER THREE

Fall

The harvest Moon has no innocence,
like the slim quarter Moon of a spring twilight,
nor has it the silver penny brilliance
of the Moon that looks down
upon the resorts of summer time.
Wise, ripe, and portly, like an old Bacchus,
it waxes night after night.

—Donald Culross Peattie

IN THE GARDEN

> A solitary maple on a woodside flames in single scarlet, recalls nothing so much as the daughter of a noble house dressed for a fancy ball, with the whole family gathered round to admire her before she goes.
>
> —Henry James

Whenever I arrive in my garden, I "make the tour." Is this a personal idiosyncrasy, or do all good gardeners do it? It would be interesting to know. By "making the tour," I mean only that I step from the front window, turn to the right, and make an infinitely detailed examination of every foot of ground, every shrub and tree, walking always over an appointed course.

There are certain very definite rules to be observed when you are "making the tour." The chief rule is that you must never take anything out of its order. You may be longing to see if a crocus has come out in the orchard, but it is strictly forbidden to look before you have inspected all the various beds, bushes, and trees that lead up to the orchard.

You must not look at the bed ahead before you have finished with the bed immediately in front of you. You may see, out of the corner of your eye, a gleam of strange and unsuspected scarlet in the next bed but one, but you must steel yourself against rushing to this exciting blaze, and you must stare with cool eyes to the earth in front, which is apparently blank, until you have made certain that it is not hiding anything. Otherwise, you will find that you rush wildly round the garden, discover one or two sensational events, and then decide that nothing else has happened.

> I would rather sit on a pumpkin and have it all to myself,
> then be crowded on a velvet cushion.
>
> —Henry David Thoreau

Attracting the Birds

I was at my mom's home in West Virginia last autumn and became mesmerized by the chickadees, juncos, and finches that came right up to the dining room window to eat from feeders attached by suction cups to the glass. I've always had bird feeders, but they were hung from trees quite a way from the house and so, while I had the inner satisfaction of doing a good deed, my eyes missed out on the pleasure of the darting creatures themselves. So I decided when I returned home to try and lure the birds to the window. I learned a bit in the process.

First, the best time to start is late fall, because the cold weather makes the birds more anxious to find food and therefore more willing to try something new. Birds' body temperatures are on average ten degrees warmer than humans, and they need an almost constant food supply to stay alive. The cold weather slows down and kills the insects they eat, so they must find an alternative food supply.

It doesn't matter which side of the house you put the feeder on, but it should be protected from the wind. You should have a good view, but it shouldn't be so busy in the room that the birds are scared off all the time. At my parents', birds would come when we were all sitting down quietly, but every time someone moved close to the window, they would scatter. A feeder on a pole in full view of the window, but back a little, turned out to be the best compromise at my house. The birds felt safer than right at the window, and I could still see them (plus cats and squirrels couldn't get the birds or seed). As for the food, wild bird seed mix is fine, as is cracked chick feed mixed with sunflower seeds for seed-eating birds. Bug eaters, such as woodpeckers, shy away from seeds, but love suet; you can buy special suet feeders at any hardware, bird, or nature store.

KITCHEN CABINET CURES: RECIPE REMEDIES

All summer you grew herbs and dried them for fall and winter, when you really need them. Many remedies can be made from what you have in the kitchen, from spices as well as herbs and plants. Here are a few simple tried-and-tested recipes handed down from generations of wise women:

Nutmeg Milk: Grated nutmeg soothes heartburn, nausea and upset tummies. Use a nutmeg grater to grate a small amount (about ⅛ teaspoon) to warmed milk (cow, soy, rice, or oat milk). Comforting and curing.

Cayenne Infusion: Use this pepper as a remedy for colds, coughs, sore throats, heartburn, hemorrhoids, and varicose veins, or as a digestive stimulant and to improve circulation. Make an infusion by adding ½ teaspoon cayenne powder to 1 cup boiled water. Add 2 cups of hot water to make a more pleasant and palatable infusion. Add lemon and honey to taste.

Catnip by the Cup: Dry a palmful of catnip leaves and steep in a cup of boiling water. Allow to steep for 5 minutes and strain as you would any loose tea. Honey helps even more, and a cup or two of catnip tea per day will have you in fine fettle, relaxed and ready. This herb is not just for kitties! We humans can also benefit from it as a remedy for upset tummies, as well as a way to diminish worry, anxiety, and nervous tension,

Cranberry Cure: How many times did your mom tell you to drink your (usually unsweetened) cranberry juice? Turns out she was right on both counts, and straight cranberry juice is very good for your bladder health and also benefits men for the prostate. Two half-cups a day, mom's orders!

Echinacea Root: Every herb store or organic grocer will have dried echinacea root for fighting colds and negating respiratory infections. Just mince a teaspoonful and steep in a cup of boiling water. Sweeten to taste and drink at least a couple of cups a day. Echinacea also makes an excellent tincture, which you can make following the how-to's herein. It is an amazing immune booster, too!

Other Herbs for Medicinal Tinctures and Teas: You can use the same basic recipe and use these plants either fresh or dried:

Lemon balm is a true aid for insomnia, anxiety, and restlessness

Licorice root is marvelous for stomach and mouth ulcers

Marshmallow, both root and leaf, strenthens gastrointestinal tract and mucus membranes

Milk thistle is excellent for the liver and kidneys

Mullein leaves help with sore throats, coughs, and chest congestion

Nettle, either fresh or dried, prevents allergies!

Slippery elm bark will get rid of heartburn, a bad cough, and sore throat

St. John's wort extract is good for depression, PMS, and hot flashes

Thyme is trusted to help with colds and congestion

SNAIL PATROL

I am a person who tries to live up to the admonition "Thou shalt not kill." From fellow humans to squirrels to even ants, I would rather try and bother an animal into changing its behavior than end its life. (The proof of my imperfection in this arises from how much I enjoy a good cut of beef or roast lamb. But that's another tale.)

As many gardeners know, as the summer heat begins to pass into the cool, wet fall, our friend the snail makes his annual food pilgrimage to many beloved plants. There are a number of ways to try and control a slimy one. For small pots, plots, and raised beds, copper tape has a slight electric current that will suggest a different meal. For larger areas, one can find many ways to kill a snail. If you happen to live near any open area, as I do, I suggest flying lessons.

For me, the easiest time to search for emerging escargot is early in the morning, as I go out to retrieve the morning paper. The garden is still fairly damp, and they are finishing up their meal. I bring an empty plastic container with me and collect all the snails I can find. Then, moving to the side of my driveway, I pick them out one by one and give them their first flight into the wild grass on the other side. As time goes on, I find fewer and fewer little helmeted ones. Maybe the first solo has scared them to death (I hope not), or maybe they have gotten my hint. I can't say for sure, but the days of finding a plant almost completely consumed by our friend the snail are gone.

> Tickle it with a hoe and it will laugh into a harvest.
>
> **—English proverb**

AUTUMNAL PLANTINGS: EXOTIC LETTUCE MIXES

Are you a buyer of those expensive (four to six dollars a pound) mixed salad greens? You can easily make your own mix by buying lettuce seeds such as Oakleaf, Black Seeded Simpson, or Red Salad Bowl, as well as arugula, mizuna, watercress, and chicory. In many parts of the country, it is too hot for lettuce during the summer—these do best in the cooler weather of fall and spring. But you can keep them going, even during the summer, if you plant new seedlings every couple of weeks and provide a "roof" of shade cloth you can buy at any garden supply store. The trick is to harvest when the leaves are very young and tender; otherwise they may be too bitter. When the plants are a couple of inches high, shear the tops with scissors for your salad; they will grow back quickly, and you will have salads for weeks.

BITTERSWEET MEMORIES

I haven't lived on the East Coast for twenty years, but I still remember feeling great anticipation, when the weather had that certain crispness and coolness and the leaves had mostly fallen, there it was—shockingly bright orange berries sitting in tiny red cups on dark brown branches. I'd come across it by surprise at the edge of the woods or in a neighbor's yard; I could never remember seeing it at any other time of the year. Whether it flowered, what the leaves were like, I couldn't say. It seemed to appear just for fall, as a feast for the birds (and for my eyes) before the long, cold winter.

> You can count the number of apples on one tree, but you can never count the number of trees in one apple.
>
> —Anonymous

SPA FENG SHUI: SAUNA SERENITY

The Scandinavians make sure their saunas have bunches of wonderfully fragrant silver birch branches hanging nearby that they can use to gently brush their skin to stimulate circulation. This sauna practice is deeply relaxing and can be a marvelous communal experience. No wonder Denmark is the happiest place on earth!

You can emulate this by hanging herbs from your shower rod or above your bathtub. This infuses the aromatic oils into the air as soon as the steam hits the herbs. We recommend bunches of lavender for tranquility and eucalyptus to aid with colds and congestion. A muslin bag filled with dried orange rind, dressed with orange essential oil, will lift depression. Rosemary can help process sadness and grief and activates your memory. A big bag of mint leaves is a major mood booster and sends concentration levels soaring. After a few uses, these herbs can be dried by laying them on a baking sheet for two weeks. Once dry, tie into a bundle with twine and use in a bonfire for the high holidays. Enjoy the holy and sweet-smelling smoke as it ascends into the heavens!

ORCHARD PLEASURES

I have always grown flowers and houseplants, so when I moved into my new house two springs ago, I was a bit taken aback by the large yard. The former owners were clearly not flower people; there was not a bloom in sight. They had planted fruit trees everywhere—several varieties of apple, an apricot, pear, cherry, and fig, and at least two kinds of plums. My first instinct was to pull them out and plant a flower bed. (The fact that they were all lined up in a row along the back fence and pressed up against my house didn't help in terms of aesthetic appeal, either.) But I couldn't imagine killing a tree and had other priorities that took my time, and so by midsummer found myself the proud owner of hundreds of green plums. Tart on the outside, with an orange, almost pumpkin-colored, sweet flesh inside, they quickly became my heart's desire. By fall, when my Macintosh apples, Bartlett pears, and figs were ripe, I was hooked. Completely organic, perfectly ripe fruit—oh, the blush on the Mac, the glow on the Bartlett—at my fingertips; it was a veritable garden of Eden. Add to that the blossoms of spring that brightened many a gray day, and I had become a rabid tree owner.

LONGEVITY ELIXIR: HOMEMADE PEAR POTION

Pears have long been prized in Asia as a lucky fruit that also offers a long and prosperous life. This pear liqueur is a special brew indeed. You will need this to make it:

- 3 large ripe pears
- 2 pods of cardamom
- Lemon peel, two inches long, half-inch wide
- Vodka, 1 quart
- 1 quart clean and sterilized Mason jar with lid (preferably dark colored glass)

Start by crushing the cardamom pods and set aside. Peel the 3 pears and cut into thin slices. Gently place the pears into the jar. Put the crushed cardamom and lemon peel on top of the pears. Cover all with the vodka. Close jar and tighten the lid, then gently shake twice. Store the jar full of pears in a dark, cool cupboard for ten days. After the ten days, remove the jar from cupboard. Pour the contents of the jar into a mixing bowl and mash thoroughly, using the back of a fork. Strain the mixture into another bowl, using a colander that has been lined with a coffee filter or cheesecloth. Repeat this process twice and then pour the pear liqueur into the

Mason jar. If you are feeling fancy, you can store in a pretty bottle, but make sure it is sterilized and seal tightly. Live long and prosper!

AUNTIE'S APPLE BRANDY SPIRITS

Here is a delightfully easy recipe that will produce a flavorful homemade liqueur that smells as good as it tastes. If you are interested in making a hassle-free bottle of spirits, apples are a wonderful way to start. Start with these ingredients:

- 4 apples, sweet ones, not sour
- 2 cups brandy
- 2 cups vodka
- 1 quart clean and sterilized Mason jar

First, clean, core, and slice your apples. Place the slices in a Mason canning jar. Pour in the alcohol to cover, using equal parts brandy and vodka. Put the jar in a cool dark place in your pantry. Allow the infusion process to happen for month, or until it is to your taste. The combination of sweet apples and brandy gives a luscious fruit-forward flavor, with no need for sugar. After infusing, strain the apple slices out, using a strainer to filter the liqueur. Pour the spirits into a pretty and sealable bottle and enjoy at your next pagan party.

Bonus tip: apples can really be used with any spirit, so let your imagination run wild!

WEATHER SIGNS

According to folklore, it will be a hard winter if: There is an unusually large crop of acorns. Heavy moss appears on the north side of trees. Grape leaves turn color early in the season. Corn has thick husks. Hornets have triple-insulated nests. Cattle get rough coats and rabbits and squirrels have heavier fur than usual. Woolly bear caterpillars are black all over. If the caterpillars are dark only in the middle, only midwinter will be hard; if the ends are darker, the beginning and the end of winter will be hard.

WALKING TO THE COMPOST PILE

We make an earnest effort to compost our kitchen waste, specifically coffee grounds, chopped-up banana skins, and other biodegradable gunk. As the compost heap is in the very back of our yard, every morning after breakfast, I wander out with a cutting board full of goodies for the little red worms. This trip necessitates a journey through the garden, and that means a step into slowed-down time.

There's always something new poking up through the top, or starting to leaf or bloom, or growing where it shouldn't, or just trimmed picturesquely with frost. For a gardener—even a hit-or-miss one like me—a walk through one's garden is almost guaranteed to provide a meditative change of pace.

> In search of my mother's garden, I found my own.
>
> —Alice Walker

Compost Considerations

Most gardeners feel that fall is the best time to start a compost heap, when leaves and other green clippings and debris are readily available. To begin, place an eight-inch-thick, even layer of wood materials, such as wood chips, sawdust, shredded newspaper, or small twigs and branches, on the bottom of your compost bin (this can be any homemade or store-bought container, at least four feet high and five feet square, with adequate but not excessive aeration, which will not be easily disturbed by woodland critters and household pets). On top of the wood layer, place an equal amount of green materials: green clippings, leaves, fruit or vegetable peelings, coffee and tea grounds, wilted cut flowers, and the like. You should never include animal flesh or by-products, eucalyptus or black walnut leaves, or anything treated with pesticides or chemicals. Gradually add enough water to make the entire contents of your compost container damp but not wet. Thoroughly mix the two layers with a long-handled shovel or rake. As new materials accumulate, they may be added: just take care to ensure that neither woods nor greens reach too high a concentration.

In approximately twelve to sixteen weeks, your compost is ready for garden use. Always take what you need from the bottom of the bin. (This will be the richest compost.)

> And forget not that the earth delights to feel your bare feet and the wind longs to play with your hair.
>
> —Kahil Gibson

WITH FAMILY AND FRIENDS

> He who shares the joy in what he's grown spreads joy abroad and doubles his own.
>
> —Anonymous

The Bridal Wreath

There was a sadly neglected corner of my parents' yard that had an ancient bedraggled shrub my mother called the bridal wreath. I thought this eyesore was undeserving of such a poetic name, since it hardly produced even a handful of white buds and seemed to have a blackberry bush rapidly overtaking it. I had recently learned the fine art of pruning and decided, one late fall afternoon, to try it on this tired old shrub. I really went at it with the shears and, with the help of my father, got rid of the blackberry invader and hacked away until not much was left of the venerable old bridal wreath. I remember my mother nearly cried when she saw the havoc we had wrought—her mother had planted this plant fifty years before. I told her not to worry, and to wait to see what happened.

It sat there all fall and winter pretty much forgotten. Then, one early spring day, we all had the most wonderful surprise—the bridal wreath had turned into a showpiece overnight, with dozens of sprays of perfect white flowers that lasted for weeks. My mother was happiest of all. Evidently the bridal wreath had been her mother's pride and joy and was now fully restored to its former glory. It was amazingly beautiful. The sprays were indeed perfect for a bridal crown.

In Memory

I was about ten years old when I asked my mother, "Why do you give people flowers when they die? Why not do it when they are alive?" This was at the annual decoration that took place at the church cemetery where my father was buried. She thoughtfully explained that the flowers are for the living. They are a symbol that we offer to sweetly remember the people we love who we have lost, and, by presenting the flowers, we have an occasion to congregate, remember, and talk about our loved ones. I noticed that day that my aunt Suzie had brought flowers from her own garden instead of the usual floral sprays. Her arrangement was a profusion of sweet William and cockscomb, carefully yet naturally arranged in a coffee tin she disguised in cellophane. The flowers reminded me of my father—a down-to-earth man who enjoyed working outside in his garden or tinkering with his tractor. Their deep crimson colors mirrored his favorite color—burgundy—the color of his only sport coat, his last truck, even the trim on our house's shutters and door. My mother was right. Those flowers were for the living.

> For in the true nature of things, if we will rightly consider, every green tree is far more glorious than if it were made of gold and silver.
>
> —Martin Luther

Trading Pleasures: Start a Flower Bulb Exchange

Start a bulb and seed exchange with friends. When you are doing your harvesting in the fall—dividing bulbs and drying our seeds for next year—try trading with friends for a no-cost way to increase the variety in your garden. We started doing this years ago, when we found out the hard way that a packet of zucchini seeds was far too many for two people to plant and eat. We divided them up among our friends around the country, and that got the ball rolling.

To send bulbs, place them in a paper bag and the bag in a box. To collect seeds, shake the flower heads over an empty glass jar. To send seeds, take a small piece of paper and make a little envelope out of it by folding it in half. Take each side and fold in about ½ inch toward the middle. Tape those two sides, place the seeds inside the opening at the top, and then fold the top down and tape again. Write on the outside what is inside, and mail in a padded envelope. A sweet surprise for family or friends.

> A violet by a mossy stone half hidden from the eye! Fair as a star, when only one is shining in the sky.
>
> —William Wordsworth

Cactus Garden

The perfect gift for those who want plants but tend to kill them from lack of water. Find a low ceramic pot or bowl and plant a few different varieties of cacti. You might want to add a pretty rock or dried flowers for color (red celosia is a wonderful choice). Handling a cactus is not painful if you wrap a towel around it several times and use the towel to lift it out of the old pot and into the new. Rather than your fingers, use a spoon to pack dirt around roots.

> I am spending delightful afternoons in my garden, watching everything living around me. As I grow older, I feel everything departing, and I love everything with more passion.
>
> —Emile Zola

Onion and Garlic Braids

I love to grow onions and garlic just so I can braid them into garlands and give them away for Christmas presents. All you have to do in preparation is to be sure to leave on the long tops when you harvest your crop. It's just like braiding hair. Cut a piece of twine as long as you want your braid to be and lay it down on a table. Line up the onions or garlic in a row on the twine with the leaves all facing toward you, each onion or garlic bulb slightly overlapping the one before. Starting with the first at the top of the line, separate the leaves into three sections, incorporating the twine into one of the sections, and braid as you would hair. When you are about halfway down the length of the first bulb's leaves, begin to incorporate the second bulb's leaves so that the bulb sits on top of the previous braid. Continue until you reach the end of the bulbs. Dry in the sun for three to five days and then they are ready for hanging as decorations—and to use. Simply snip off the last one on the braid as needed.

Great Gift: Tie up a package of sunflower seeds with a ribbon and a sunflower.

Gardening Cohorts

I'm part of a group of eight friends who live in neighboring towns and have gotten together at least once a month for the past four years. We find we often function like old-fashioned barn-raising neighbors—when someone needs to move, we're all there hauling boxes; we have summer solstice celebrations and sixteenth-birthday celebrations and adoption parties. A lot of our sharing is around our gardens. When a massive oak in our yard died, we divided the firewood among us; when a rhododendron bush needed lifting up, the rhododendron expert among us was in charge. We swap trees, give produce, offer orchids, help out when it's time to weed or harvest, trade recipes, and visit nurseries together. Nothing unusual, except in the fast-paced, mobile, urban life, when neighbors seem to come and go in the blink of an eye, it's the kind of connection that I find all too rarely. No reason to be together, except the sharing of the dailiness of life on an ongoing basis. A lot like nature. Very ordinary, but profoundly important.

> Remember that the most beautiful things in the world are the most useless, peacocks and lilies for instance.
>
> —John Ruskin

Worm Garden

This is an activity more likely to be enjoyed by the little ones. Fill a gallon glass jar with alternating layers of sand and garden soil until it is almost full. Then add compost items, such as coffee grounds, banana peels cut into pieces, old dried leaves, etc. Place about ten worms on the top and cover with a piece of black cloth. Whenever curiosity strikes, remove the cloth for a few minutes and see what the worms are up to. When interest wanes, return worms to the garden.

Legacy of Trees

Our family has decided to plant three trees, representing our three family members, in each of the fifty states. The places we're picking are all places that contain either our last name or one of our first names. We're doing it because we believe planting trees is a way to help protect and beautify nature, as well as provide habitat for birds and animals. So far we've done twenty states and have been received graciously in each town. We generally find a family that is willing to have us plant a tree in their yard, but we've also done a few street trees.

> I lie amid the Goldenrod.
> I love to see it lean and nod.
>
> **—Mary Clemmer**

THE GIVING TREE

In Celtic lore, certain kinds of trees were called wishing trees. Taoists refer to them as money trees; either way, they can be giving trees. Choose from among these magical trees, or trust your intuition in arboreal matters:

- Willow—for healing broken hearts
- Apple—for divination
- Cherry—for romance
- Oak—for strength and sensuality
- Peach—for love
- Olive—for peace
- Aspen—for sensitivity
- Eucalyptus—for purification

Gather together:

- **Plain white piece of paper**
- **Pen**

Write your wishes for prosperity and luck on the paper. Specificity is key, and you should include the details of what you are asking for. If you need more money to buy a new laptop, write that down and it can be more than one wish. Now, fold the paper as small as possible and bury it in the soil by the bottom of the tree. Every time you water your giving tree, you will be helping your wish come true!

IN AUNT RUTH'S GARDEN

As a child, I was fortunate enough to have an aunt who loved to garden. She had a beautiful old-fashioned garden in the Ohio Valley with many plants that had been handed down through generations of my family. I can still smell the lilac from a bush that was over one hundred years old and home to many bees. When I was barely old enough to toddle along behind her, Aunt Ruth would show me her tricks of the trade—rooting, transplanting, deadheading, even grafting.

I quickly learned that, by admiring one of my aunt's flowers heartily, I would be given a seedling, a cutting, or a whole plant. In her infinite wisdom, she decided that I could be taught the craft of gardening and help her clean and thin some beds at the same time. This became a marvelous arrangement that persisted well into my adulthood, until I moved three thousand miles away to a different "zone." Now, as a city dweller, my dream is to have a little garden patch of my own where I can carry on the family tradition.

HERBAL AMULETS: HANDMADE GIFTS OF CARING AND CURING

You will experience years of enjoyment from tending your garden, as Voltaire taught us in his masterpiece, *Candide*. You can share that pleasure with your friends and those you love through gifts from your garden. Your good intentions will be returned many times over. I keep a stock of small muslin drawstring bags for creating amulets. If you are a crafty person, you can make the bags, sewing by hand, and stuff the dried herbs inside.

- **For courage and heart**: mullein or borage
- **For good cheer**: nettle or yarrow
- **For friends**: ivy, broomstraw, and maidenhair fern
- **For safe travels**: comfrey
- **For fertility**: cyclamen or mistletoe
- **For protection from deceit**: snapdragon
- **For good health**: rue
- **For success**: woodruff
- **For strength**: mugwort
- **For youthful looks**: an acorn

Amulets should be kept on your person at all times, in a pocket, in your purse or book bag, or on a string around your neck.

BURST OF FLAVOR

My husband is a rabid tomato grower. After our enthusiasm for freshly picked and eaten cherry tomatoes has waned and fall has arrived, then it's time for sun-dried tomatoes. Though I have actually dried tomatoes in the sun, a much more dependable and efficient method is to dry them in an oven for 5 to 8 hours, depending on the size of the fruit. After cleaning and splitting the tomatoes in half, I salt them lightly on oiled cooking pans and place them in a 170°F oven. When they are dry but not crispy, I pack jars with the tomatoes and fill to the top with extra-virgin olive oil (press with a spoon to make sure the air is all out and add some more oil if needed to cover tomatoes completely). We have so many we give a lot away, but I always save some for ourselves. In the middle of winter, these make the quickest and sweetest tomato paste in the world.

> More than anything, I must have flowers, always, always.
>
> —Claude Monet

Good and Green Tomato Pickles

Here's my grandmother's answer as to what to do with all those green tomatoes in your garden that will never turn red because frost is coming. It can be cut down proportionally. If you have never canned anything before, be sure to read about the process in a basic cookbook like *Joy of Cooking*.

One dry quart green tomatoes (1 dry quart is 1/6 larger than a liquid one, says *Joy of Cooking*)

- 2 large onions
- ½ cup plus 1 ⅓ teaspoon salt
- 3 cups vinegar
- 3 red peppers, seeded and chopped
- 3 green peppers, seeded and chopped
- 3 cloves garlic, chopped not pressed
- 1 ½ teaspoons dry mustard
- 1 ½ teaspoons whole cloves
- 1 tablespoon ground ginger
- 1 ½ teaspoons celery seed

Slice green tomatoes and onions thinly. Sprinkle with ½ cup of salt and let stand overnight. Rinse and drain.

Boil the vinegar, add the peppers and garlic, and boil vigorously for 1 minute. Add the tomatoes, onions, and remaining ingredients and simmer slowly for 20 minutes. Pack while hot into hot, sterilized canning jars and seal immediately with hot, sterilized caps. Process in hot-water bath 5 minutes. Makes about 5 to 6 pints.

Sun-Dried Tomato Poulet

This recipe never fails to get raves at parties large and small. It's simple, once you get the hang of the rolling-up process. I pound the chicken with a full wine bottle, but you can use a flat mallet instead.

- 4 skinless, boneless chicken breasts
- Waxed paper
- ½ cup sun-dried tomatoes packed in oil, drained and chopped
- 4 ounces goat cheese
- 2 tablespoons chopped fresh basil
- 2 tablespoons olive oil
- ½ cup chicken broth or white wine

Place the breasts, one at a time, between two sheets of waxed paper on a flat surface. Pound until ¼ inch thick. (You may go through several pieces of waxed paper.)

Spread 1 ounce of goat cheese on each chicken breast. Top each with 1 tablespoon sun-dried tomatoes and 1 teaspoon basil. (There will be some of each left over.) Roll up like a jelly roll and secure with toothpicks so that no filling is showing.

Heat the oil in a large skillet over a medium flame and add the chicken, turning frequently until white inside and lightly browned on the outside. Be sure the inside is thoroughly cooked—this takes 12 to 15 minutes. Remove and set aside on a warm plate. Cover with aluminum foil.

Add the broth or wine and the remaining sun-dried tomatoes and basil. Turn up heat to high and reduce liquid by half. Remove toothpicks from chicken and pour sauce over rollups. Serves four.

OCEANS OF OREGANO

Once you get the oregano going, there's no stopping it from spreading its tender branches several feet in all directions. By the end of the season, my husband and I just clip it back and hang it in the drying shed. When it's dry, we fill old jars and give them to our non-gardening friends. There's nothing finer than homemade pizza dough, covered with homemade sauce and topped with homegrown oregano.

> Dear common flower, that grow'st beside the way,
> fringing the dusty road with harmless gold.
>
> —James Russell Lowell

BOUQUET GARNI

Many recipes I make call for bouquet garni and, before I had an herb garden, it used to drive me crazy—who has one sprig of chervil lying around? Now I just walk out to the garden and pick exactly the amount I need. If you want to use dried herbs, you can make a number of these and store in an airtight container.

- Cheesecloth
- 4 sprigs fresh parsley or 1 teaspoon dried
- 2 sprigs fresh thyme or 1 teaspoon dried
- 1 bay leaf
- 1 sprig chervil or 1 teaspoon dried
- One sprig marjoram or 1 teaspoon dried
- Kitchen string

Fold the cheesecloth twice to make three layers and then cut into a 4-inch square. Place herbs onto square of cloth. Bundle up the sides and tie with string. Makes one.

MARIGOLD BUNS

- ½ cup sugar
- 1 stick butter
- 2 eggs
- 3 cups flour
- 3 teaspoons baking powder
- 2 tablespoons apple juice
- Petals from three marigolds (also known as calendula), washed

Preheat oven to 350°F. Cream sugar and butter together in a large bowl. Add eggs and beat until creamy. Sift the flour and baking powder together and combine with sugar mixture, adding apple juice, until well beaten. Stir in marigold petals.

Grease a cookie sheet and drop mixture by spoonful onto prepared sheet. Bake for 10 minutes or until lightly browned. Makes 2 dozen.

CORN MOON FALL CHOWDER

Here's a delicious chowder for those cool, early fall evenings at the end of the corn season.

- 1 red pepper, diced
- 6 cups chicken broth
- kernels from 8 ears of corn
- 1 russet potato, peeled and cubed
- 1 quart low-fat milk
- ¼ pound bacon, fat trimmed, cut into ¼ inch pieces
- 1 large onion, diced
- salt and pepper to taste
- 5 tablespoons chopped fresh parsley
- 2 tablespoons chopped fresh dill
- ½ cup slivered fresh basil leaves

Blanch the bell pepper in boiling water for 1 minute. Drain and set aside.

Place chicken broth in large soup pot and add half the corn and the potato. Bring to a boil, reduce heat to medium, cover and cook until potatoes are tender, about 10 to 15 minutes. Let cool slightly. Puree in batches, in a blender or processor, until just smooth. Transfer to a large bowl and stir in milk.

Sauté bacon in the soup pot over low heat just until fat renders out, about 5 minutes. Add reserved puree, zucchini, and remaining corn kernels. Season with salt and pepper and cook for 5 to 8 minutes (do not boil). Stir in blanched bell pepper and all herbs. Serves six.

HOMEGROWN CELERY

I am addicted to growing celery. Unlike onions or broccoli, celery is a completely different creature than the store-bought variety. It is deep green and the flavor is five times as strong as its pale cousin's. I love to pick a few stalks at a time instead of having to buy the whole plant and then letting it rot in the bin.

Celery Salad

- This is modified from an old Shaker recipe.
- 3 cups sliced celery
- ¼ cup olive oil
- ¼ cup cider vinegar
- ½ teaspoon sugar
- salt and pepper to taste
- 1 teaspoon chopped chives
- 1 tablespoon capers

Bring a pot of water to boil and add the celery. Cook until tender, about 2 to 3 minutes. Drain and place celery in a bowl. In a small bowl, combine the oil, vinegar, sugar, salt, and pepper and pour over the celery while still warm. Chill. Just before serving, add the chives and capers. Serves six.

A THORNY PLEASURE

We have a scramble of blackberry bushes along our side-yard fence that are volunteers from the streets' edge around our neighborhood. They are a painful problem—nothing can kill them, at least nothing I am willing to use—that I have mostly ignored, but as summer waned into fall, I decided to stop resisting and start enjoying the inevitable. So my husband and I got our containers and went blackberry picking around our neighborhood. Naturally we ate a fair number, but we ended up with enough for about a dozen jars of jam. I've been surprised at how much pleasure each jar has brought me—my very own homemade jam.

Blackberry Jam

This works especially well with any berries. Quantity depends on how many berries you've picked. Sometimes this comes out a bit runny, so if you're nervous, use pectin and follow the directions on the box.

- Hulled and washed berries
- Sugar

Weigh the berries and then weigh out an equal amount of sugar. Mash berries, place in a non-aluminum pan, and slowly bring to a boil, stirring often. Add sugar and simmer until thick, stirring often so bottom doesn't burn. Pour into clean hot jars with sealing lids and process in a hot-water bath (see a general cookbook if you don't know how to do this) for 5 minutes.

> A morning glory at my window satisfies me more than the metaphysics of books.
>
> —Walt Whitman

Blackberry Malt Vinegar

Blackberries are one of life's sweetest gifts, growing abundantly in the bramble along the rambling path. An extremely effective medicinal tonic can be made by soaking a quart of berries in a quart of malt vinegar for three days. Drain and strain the liquid into a pan. Simmer and stir in sugar, one pound to every two cups of tonic. Boil gently for five minutes and skim off any foam. Cool and pour into a sealable jar. This potion is so powerful; you can add a teaspoon into a cup of water and cure tummy aches, cramps, fevers, coughs, and colds. Best of all, blackberry vinegar is both a medicine and a highly prized dessert topping in the UK. Pour some over your apple pie and cream and you will soon scurry off to pick blackberries all summer.

Summer Sweet Blackberry Jam

Below is a tried-and-true recipe for a simple berry jam. Our family favorite is blackberries, as the color is nearly as delicious as the taste when spread on warm toast. You'll need the following:

- 2 cups blackberries (or try raspberries or strawberries)
- 2 cups sugar
- 2 teaspoons lemon juice
- 1 slice of lemon rind
- Apple slice
- Canning jars and tongs

Crush the berries with a potato masher, softly, not too hard. Place all the ingredients in a stockpot and boil over high heat for 5 minutes, stirring the mixture to prevent it from sticking or burning. Reduce the heat to medium-high and continue to boil and stir. Remove any foam with a large spoon. After a half-hour, the jam will begin to thicken up. If your jam is setting slowly, you can add more lemon juice or a slice of apple. Pectin, which is regularly used thicken jams and jellies, is made from apples. Thus, a slice of apple will serve the same purpose.

When the jam is ready, pour it into sterilized jars. The jars should be warm when the jam is added, so keep the sterilized articles in the oven, dishwasher, or canning water bath until you need them; ditto the lids and rings. Make sure to leave a generous ½-inch gap between the jam and the top of the jar—this is known as headspace in the world of jam. Place the lids on the jars and screw them on firmly.

Place the sealed jars into the water bath and cover with at least an inch of water. Boil for 10 minutes. Using jar tongs, lift the jars out and let them cool at room temperature. You will hear the lids seal when they make a popping noise as the domed lid is sucked down. Processed jam will last at least a year and makes a lovely gift. For small batches, you can make your jam and store it in the fridge as soon as it has cooled off. Berries contain protection magic as well as that of abundance. Folklore says vampires are afraid of blackberry vines.

STRAWBERRY FIELDS JAM

July is one of the sweetest times to enjoy your garden, and strawberries are a harbinger of the good summer times ahead. To make this lucky jam, get the following ingredients:

- 5 cups of strawberries
- 1 teaspoon unsalted butter
- 1 ¾ ounces powdered fruit pectin
- 7 cups granulated sugar
- ½ cup fresh basil, chopped
- 9 clean and sterilized 1-pint canning jars

Macerate the strawberries in a big bowl. In a large pot, melt the butter and pour in the crushed strawberries. Fold in the powdered pectin. Heat the mixture to a full boil over high heat, stirring constantly. Add in the sugar and bring again to a full rolling boil. Boil and stir for 1 more minute. Now, add in the chopped basil.

Remove the pot from heat and skim off any foam. Ladle the hot mixture into nine half-pint jars, leaving ¼ inch at the top. Look for and remove any air bubbles. If you need to fill in, add in more hot jam mixture. Carefully wipe the jar rims, then seal the lids on the jars. Place jars into canner with simmering water, ensuring that they are completely covered with water. Bring to a boil; process for 10 minutes. Remove jars and cool. Strawberries are widely regarded as an aphrodisiac, and basil brings money to your house. Making this "Love and Money Jam" will be a great gift to everyone in your household and anyone who is served this jolliest of jams.

HOMEMADE INFUSED VINEGARS

Before the herbs die back in your garden, why not use them to make homemade vinegars? Packaged in pretty bottles, they make a unique gift. Pick and wash the herbs to be used (long sprigs of basil, rosemary, thyme, sage, or a combination all work well and look beautiful in the bottles). Dried herbs will not work as well. The rule of thumb is one cup of fresh herbs per quart of vinegar. Dry them well on paper towels. Pack the herbs into clean bottles or jars with lids or corks, and fill with white vinegar that has been heated to a pre-boil. Cook or cap. Stand the jars on a sunny windowsill for about two weeks (four weeks if not very sunny). The warmth of the sun will infuse the vinegar with the herbs. Taste test. If it doesn't seem flavorful enough, strain vinegar and add more herbs. When it suits you, label and decorate the jars with a beautiful ribbon. Store at room temperature.

For a more lively infusion, try chili garlic vinegar; as many dried whole red chilies as will fit in your bottle, a tablespoon of slightly crushed whole peppercorns, five slightly crushed garlic cloves, and a few sprigs of thyme. Again, fill the bottles, pour the heated white wine vinegar in, and cap.

Herbal Alchemy: Perfect Plants for DIY Vinegars

The leaves and stalks of these plants are very good for making herbal vinegars: apple mint, basil, catnip, garlic mustard, orange mint, peppermint, rosemary, spearmint, thyme, and yarrow.

Dill and fennel seeds work very well, as do lemon and orange peels.

The flowers of bee balm, chives, goldenrod, lavender, and yarrow work well.

Roots also infuse nicely into herbal vinegars—the best are dandelion, chicory, ginger, garlic, mugwort, and burdock.

GARLIC SPREAD

This is really a confit. Slather it on sourdough baguettes or use it any time a recipe calls for cooked garlic. And don't forget to use the leftover garlic-infused oil. If you have a large garlic crop or make a trip to the farmers' market, you can package this up in gift jars for friends as well as yourself.

- 8 ounces garlic cloves, peeled
- 2 cups olive oil
- sterilized jars with lids that seal

In a medium saucepan, place the garlic and oil. Bring to simmer and cook over low heat for 25 to 30 minutes or until garlic is very tender. Cool and pack into containers. Store in refrigerator and use within two weeks. Makes 2 pounds.

> Some persons may think that flowers are things of no use; that they are nonsensical things. The same may be, and perhaps with more reason, said of pictures. An Italian, while he gives his fortune for a picture, will laugh to scorn a Hollander, who leaves a tulip-root as a fortune to his son. For my part, as a thing to keep and not to sell: as a thing, the possession of which is to give me pleasure, I hesitate not a moment to prefer the plant of a fine carnation to a gold watch set with diamonds.
>
> —William Cobbett

COZINESS BY THE CUP: AMBROSIAL BREWS

Herbal tea conjures a very powerful alchemy because, when you drink it, you take the healing inside. For an ambrosial brew with the power to calm any storm, add a sliver of ginger root and a pinch each of chamomile and peppermint to a cup of hot black tea.

Herbal teas can also nourish the soul and heal the body:

Blueberry leaf tea: Reduces mood swings, evens glucose levels, and helps varicose veins.

Nettle: Raises the energy level, boosts the immune system, and is packed with iron and vitamins.

Fennel: Awakens and uplifts, freshens the breath, and aids colon health.

Echinacea: Lends an increased and consistent sense of well-being and prevents colds and flu.

Ginger root: Calms and cheers while aiding digestion, nausea, and circulation.

Dandelion root: Grounds and centers, provides many minerals and nutrients, and cleanses the liver of toxins.

Basil, Mint, and Rose Hip Tea

- 12 ounces water
- 2 tablespoons chopped fresh spearmint
- 2 tablespoons chopped fresh basil
- 2 rose hip tea bags
- honey or sugar to taste (optional)

Place the water, spearmint, and basil in a non-reactive pan. Cover and bring the water to a rolling boil. Remove lid, stir, then add the tea bags. Steep covered for 5 minutes. Strain tea into 2 warmed cups. Sweeten with honey or sugar, if desired. Serves two.

Give Your Plants a Cup of Tea

Don't throw leftover herbal tea away—use it to water your houseplants. But be sure it is caffeine-free; plants like tea, as long as it is unleaded.

PICKLED CRAB APPLES

You can use homegrown or store-bought crab apples for this.

- 1 quart apple cider vinegar
- 3 pounds brown sugar
- 1 tablespoon whole cloves
- 1 stick cinnamon
- 1 teaspoon ginger
- 1 teaspoon nutmeg
- 3 gallons crab apples, washed, blossom ends and stems removed

Bring all ingredients except apples to a boil. Add apples and cook until apples are tender but not mushy, about 10 to 15 minutes, depending on size. Remove apples, place them in sterilized jars, and pour syrup over. Seal. Makes about 2 gallons.

LAVENDER KISSES

- 1 cup granulated sugar
- ¼ cup dried lavender flowers
- 1 ½ cups confectioners' sugar
- 6 egg whites, at room temperature
- Cool Whip or whipped cream, optional

Preheat oven to 225°. Combine the granulated sugar and the lavender in a food processor until pulverized. Sift into a bowl with the confectioners' sugar. In a large bowl, beat the egg whites with an electric mixer until soft peaks form, then gradually add the sugar mixture, beating until soft peaks form.

Place a sheet of aluminum foil over a cookie sheet and drop mixture by spoonfuls onto sheet an inch apart. Flatten out a bit and bake about two hours. Kisses should be crisp but still pastel blue. Cool. Eat as is, or sandwich 2 together with Cool Whip or whipped cream. Makes 3 dozen.

THANKSGIVING PUMPKIN MUFFINS

You don't have to grow your own pumpkins for these, but if you do, follow a basic recipe for cooking mashed pumpkin and then proceed.

- 1 large egg
- ½ cup melted butter
- ½ cup milk
- 1 cup canned pumpkin
- 1 ¾ cups all-purpose flour
- 1 cup packed brown sugar
- 1 teaspoon ground ginger
- 1 teaspoon baking soda
- 1 teaspoon cinnamon
- ¼ teaspoon nutmeg
- ¼ teaspoon salt

Ginger Crunch Topping

- ½ cup all-purpose flour
- ¼ cup brown sugar
- ¼ cup finely chopped candied ginger
- ¼ cup butter

Making the muffins: Break egg into a bowl and whisk in the melted butter and milk. Add pumpkin and whisk until blended. Stir in flour, brown sugar, baking soda, ginger, cinnamon, nutmeg, and salt into butter mixture. Stir until just blended. Divide batter between 12 paper-lined muffin tins.

To make the topping: Using a fork, mix together flour, brown sugar, candied ginger, and butter until crumbly. Sprinkle evenly over the tops of the muffins.

Bake at 350° until cake tester inserted into the center comes out clean, about 25 minutes. Makes 1 dozen.

PUMPKIN SAGE SOUP

- 2 teaspoons olive oil
- 2 large onions, chopped
- 3 pounds pumpkin, seeded, peeled, and diced, or 1 large container canned pumpkin
- 3 garlic cloves, peeled and chopped
- 1 cup cooked rice
- 1 teaspoon fresh sage, minced
- 2 teaspoons salt (to taste)
- 1 teaspoon ground white pepper
- 4 cups water, approximately
- minced parsley

Heat olive oil in a large heavy stock pot. Add onions and cook about 5 minutes on medium/high heat. Add raw pumpkin and garlic, and cook for 20 minutes, stirring frequently until pumpkin is tender. (If you are using cooked pumpkin, add with the water and rice.) Add water, rice, sage, salt, and pepper. Stir well and cook for 10 minutes to meld the flavors. Puree the soup in a food processor. Check the seasoning and consistency. Add more water if necessary. Garnish with minced parsley. Serve piping hot. Serves six.

CRANBERRY-PEAR RELISH

Here's a tasty variation on the old Thanksgiving standby: cranberry sauce. It never fails to win raves when I make it. Don't be afraid of the jalapenos, they just give it a zing.

- 1 tablespoon vegetable oil
- ½ onion, diced
- 1 ½ teaspoons minced ginger
- 2 garlic cloves, minced
- 1 large jalapeno, minced
- ½ cup red wine
- ⅓ cup vinegar
- 1 cup brown sugar
- 1 teaspoon pepper
- 1 teaspoon cinnamon
- ½ tablespoon each allspice, ground cloves, ground coriander, and ground nutmeg
- ½ teaspoon dried thyme
- 3 cups fresh cranberries
- 3 pears, peeled and diced
- ½ cup raisins
- ¼ cup maple syrup

In a large saucepan, heat the oil and add the onion, ginger, garlic, and jalapeno. Cook, stirring, over medium heat until onion is tender, about 5 minutes. Add the wine, vinegar, brown sugar, and spices, and simmer, stirring occasionally, until syrupy, about 20 minutes.

Add remaining ingredients and simmer until cranberries are cooked, about 10 minutes. Serve at room temperature. Serves six.

> Natural objects themselves, even when they make no claim to beauty, excite the feelings, and occupy the imagination. Nature pleases, attracts, delights, merely because it is nature. We recognize in it an Infinite Power.
>
> —Karl Wilhelm Humboldt

ARTFUL ARRANGEMENTS

You don't need a flower garden to create beautiful arrangements. All you need is access to a field and a bit of imagination. Wild Queen Anne's lace, bittersweet, winter cress, sea grape leaves, chive flowers, wild mustard, thistles, horsetails, and goldenrod all look wonderful in a simple vase, either all one variety, or in combination. Even the simplicity of dried grasses or bare willow branches can be beautiful, while various seed pods, when dried, can make extraordinary decorations.

> My heart and I lie small upon the earth like a grain of throbbing sand.
>
> —Zitkala-Sa

Lighting the Way: Potted Candles

- bendable dry floral foam
- six-inch terra-cotta pot
- four-inch diameter candle
- floral wire
- solidago (goldenrod)
- lavender
- larkspur
- miniature roses
- moss

Take the floral foam and cut a piece to fit inside the pot with about three inches of foam above the rim. Cut off the top four corners at a 45-degree angle. Push the foam down into the pot and then push the candle into the foam.

Make eight small bunches each of solidago and lavender, and wire each bunch with floral wire. Beginning with the solidago, push the bunches into the foam on opposite sides to maintain a balance. The lavender bunches go in next in the spaces between the solidago. Move higher and lower as you go to create a thick ring of material.

Make several small, shorter bunches each of larkspur and roses and add them randomly filling all small gaps. Rotate the pot as you work to notice how the flowers look from different angles.

When you are satisfied with the arrangement of the flowers, take some roses and place moss around the base of the candle to cover the foam.

HARVESTING TIME: HERBS

Fall is the time to harvest the herbs you've been growing all summer for wreaths, potpourri, and other flower crafts. The best time to harvest herbs is a sunny morning after the dew has evaporated. Be sure to pick at their peak—and only the amount you can dry at once.

To dry herbs in bunches, start with a lot of stems of herbs like mint, angelica, artemisia, yarrow, and goldenrod. Gather in small bunches, tie the ends with string, and hang upside down in a cool, dark place, like the attic or basement or garage, and far enough apart so the air will circulate around it. An older age bed or even a closet will do. Sun or bright light will leach out the color. If you hang them in the kitchen, be sure to keep them out of range of the sink and stove, where moisture will prevent them from drying. To dry petals and leaves, scatter in a single layer on a drying tray or window screen and place where air can circulate freely around the pan. Leave for two to ten days; they are ready when leaves are brittle. If space and time are a consideration, try the microwave method.

Microwave Herb Drying

You can easily dry and preserve your own herbs at home, either those you've grown yourself or store-bought ones. Rinse freshly picked leaves (remove the stems) and air-dry. Spread 2 cups of leaves in a single layer on a bed of paper towels in the microwave. Microwave on high for 4 to 6 minutes (drying time will vary according to the machine, so monitor carefully!). Cool the leaves completely before storing in an airtight container out of direct sunlight.

Healing Spices

Did you know your pantry is like a pharmacy? Thankfully, it is far cheaper. *Cumin* is loaded with phytochemicals, antioxidants, iron, copper, calcium, potassium, manganese, selenium, zinc, and magnesium, and contains high amounts of B-complex. Cumin helps with insomnia. *Cinnamon* is truly a power spice. Just half a teaspoon daily can dramatically reduce blood glucose levels in those with type 2 diabetes and lower cholesterol. *Cayenne* promotes circulation and boosts metabolism. *Clove* is an antifungal and eases toothaches. Nutrient-rich *parsley* is a detoxifying herb and acts as an anti-inflammatory and anti-spasmodic, helping conditions from colic to indigestion. Rub it on itchy skin for instant relief! *Sage* is very beneficial in treating gum and throat infections. Sage tea has helped ease depression and anxiety for generations. *Thyme* is a cure for a hangover and doubles to alleviate colds and bronchitis. *Cilantro* is a good source of iron, magnesium, phytonutrients, and flavonoids, and is also high in dietary fiber. Cilantro has been used for thousands of years as a digestive, lowering blood sugar, possibly the result of stimulating insulin secretion. *Ginger* stimulates circulation and is an excellent digestive, aiding in absorption of food, and rids bloat. Immune champion *turmeric* boosts production of antioxidants and reduces of inflammation. Blue Zone centenarians credit their long healthy lives to drinking turmeric-root tea daily. Pack your pantry with these seasonings for optimal health and happiness.

> One day with life and heart is more than time enough to find a world.
>
> —James Russell Lowell

SIMPLY WONDERFUL DIY WREATHS

You can easily make any kind of wreath—bay leaf, evergreen, dried flowers, etc.—once you learn the basic technique:

Buy a glue gun, florist wire, and a wire ring frame in the size you want from a floral supply store. (Take into account that the finished wreath will be several inches larger than the frame.)

Decide on your base herb. Make sure it is long-stemmed, already dried in small bunches, and that you have enough to cover the frame. Lavender, thyme, santolina, and silver king artemisia are all good. The rest of your choices will be accents. Be sure to handle the herbs and flowers gently; they are fragile.

Spread the bunches of herbs over the frame so that it is completely covered, all overlapping in the same direction, so that the stem of the previous bunch doesn't show, and attach to the frame with florist wire. This becomes your base.

Take smaller pieces of the same base material and tuck them around the inner and outer edges, with sprigs all going in the same direction, until it is filled in the shape you want.

Now take your accent flowers and place them onto the front of the base in a pleasing arrangement. Yarrow, lavender, goldenrod, and statice are good for a basic dried flower wreath; chives, marjoram, mint, and sage work well for the culinary herbal wreath. Once they are in the right place, glue them with a glue gun. You can also attach cinnamon sticks, garlic bulbs, etc., by wiring them to floral picks and then sticking them into the wreath.

BAY LEAF RING OF PLENTY

After the first rains of November, when all the leaves are rinsed of dust, the bay laurels begin to flower in small clusters. This is the time when I get ready for my holiday bay-leaf wreath-making. In my own kitchen, I have used the same ten-inch steel ring for years. Before making a new wreath, I unwind the old wire and do a ritual burning of last year's leaves in the fireplace. Though the leaves are brittle, they still spark with the heavy oils that remain. Then it's time to gather a couple of big bags of clipped branches with the freshest, cleanest leaves. (I suggest you do this phase outside on a picnic table, since the smell of fresh bay leaves can be overwhelming. Plus, this outdoor processing gives the spiders a chance to find new homes.) Then simply wind thin-gauge wire around a few bunches at a time as you attach them to the heavy wire ring. For a week or two, you may cry every time you enter the kitchen. This may be because you are affected by holiday sentiments, or it may mean you are very sensitive to the intense oils vaporizing from your year's supply of bay leaves hanging over your oven.

> I can enjoy flowers quite happily without translating them into Latin.
>
> **—Cornelius Otis Skimmer**

PRESSED FLOWERS

Making pressed flowers is incredibly easy. It requires no special equipment and costs absolutely nothing. Here's how: when your new telephone book comes, save the old one and put it somewhere where you won't lose it. Find a meadow and collect small bouquets of wildflowers. Lay them flat in different parts of the phone book. Place a small boulder, or anything else that's heavy and not likely to take off, on top of the phone book. Let sit for a few months.

> The kiss of sun for pardon; the song of the birds for mirth—One is nearer God's heart in a garden than anywhere else on earth.
>
> —Dorothy Gurney

Floral Napkin Rings

At the craft store, buy a set of clear Lucite napkin rings (the kind with an opening that allows you to put a piece of paper inside). Cut paper to fit inside the rings. Glue pressed flowers in any pleasing arrangement onto the paper, and cover the paper with clear, heavy tape, like that used for sending packages. Insert the paper into the rings. If you can't find Lucite napkin rings, you can glue pressed flowers directly onto wooden rings, then give them several coats of shellac.

Sending Love: Make Your Own Greeting Cards

Place pressed flowers in a pattern you like on the fronts of blank cards or on stiff artists' paper you can get at a craft or variety store. Attach them to the paper with a dab of glue. Take an appropriate amount of transparent, self-stick plastic film (like contact paper) from the roll and carefully place on top of the flowers, pressing from the center to the edge to eliminate air bubbles. Trim the edge of the plastic to fit the paper. You can then send them to your friends for Christmas, birthdays, Valentine's Day, or no reason at all. Bookmarks can be made in exactly the same way—just cut the paper to an appropriate size.

> My garden, with its silence and pulses of fragrance that come and go on the airy undulations, affects me like sweet music. Care stops at the gates, and gazes at me wistfully through the bars.
>
> —Alexander Smith

Pressed Flower Paperweights

These are truly a simple pleasure. After your pressed flowers are ready, buy a hollow glass mold at a craft store. Trace the bottom of the mold onto a piece of mat board. Cut out the mat, arrange the pressed flowers on it, then glue flowers in place. Hot glue the glass mold to the mat, when dry, glue a circle of a circle of felt to the bottom.

Dried Flower Basket

If you are just starting to create craft pieces for your home, try this easy idea. One advantage for beginners is that you can take the flowers out as many times as necessary to get the right look.

- Chicken wire
- Medium-sized wicker basket
- Amaranthus
- A variety of other tall, relatively straight dried flowers (larkspur, roses, and lavender are all good)

Take the chicken wire and cut it into a circle two to three times the size of the basket opening. Form it into a flattened ball slightly larger than the basket opening and place it in the basket, filling up the whole inside. Take the Amaranthus and place enough of this plant into the basket to hide most of the top of the wire, but still leave room for the other flowers. (Make sure the stems go to the bottom.)

Place the other flowers into the basket one type at a time. Balance the placement as you go so that when the arrangement is finished, no one type is bunched together.

Take the basket to the place it will occupy in your home and look at it from all angles. (This piece is particularly nice on the floor by the fireplace, but any low bench or shelf will do too.) Notice how the flowers are balanced and make any adjustments that seem necessary.

Fragrant Fires

You can bundle up mini-logs of assorted dried flowers to add fragrance to fires. Simply gather up an assortment of dried flowers and herbs still on the stems. Make into bunches about eight inches long and as big around as your fist. Tie each bundle with brown jute or raffia. When your fire is smoldering, tip with a flower log and enjoy the fragrance.

To make a hearth decoration, tie four or five bundles in a row and cut the stems down to the same length. Take a length of jute three times as long as you want the finished hanging to be. Fold jute in half. Place one bundle in the fold. Grasp both sides of the twine and securely tie the bundle with a simple overhand knot. Move two inches up the jute and tie another simple knot. This becomes the bottom point for the next bundle. Again tie the bundle. Continue until you've used all the bundles. You should have twelve inches or so of jute left at top. Fold that down in half and securely tie to the topmost knot. This becomes the hanger.

Dried Flower Swag

- Dried greens such as eucalyptus, rye, or other greens
- Dried flowers such as strawflowers, baby's breath, geranium, etc.
- Floral wire
- Wire cutters
- Glue gun
- 3 feet of three-inch wired ribbon

Take the dried greens and create two bunches—the more, the bigger the swag. Intermingle the stems of the two bunches to create what looks like a bow tie. Wrap this in the center several times with the floral wire until it is fairly secure. Take the glue gun and squirt glue into the center to help hold the bundle together.

Take the dried flowers and wire and glue them onto the swag, one type at a time. Balance the types as you go and glue into the center three inches. When you have put on as many types as you as you want, wrap the center with three or four turns of wire. Twist the ends together and cut off the excess. Wrap over this with the ribbon, hiding the wire and glue, and trim to desired length. (If you want a more rustic look, use up to two dozen or so strands of raffia.) Create a wire hanger in the back by wrapping floral wire, on the back side of the swag, through and around the ribbon and wire, creating a loop. Hang from wire in the back.

NOURISHING BODY AND SOUL

> When the world wearies, and society ceases to satisfy, there is always the garden.
>
> —Minnie Aumonier

Pondering the Potato: Back to Basics

It is early fall, and I stand surveying the wonderful harvest of tomatoes, cucumbers, string beans, Swiss chard, onions, zucchini, and garlic that I grew single-handedly. As a man who grew up in the slums of Boston, the ability to grow food on my own land has always been deeply meaningful to me. This bounty, however, is not what gives me the most gratifying moment in my garden. It is what I hold in my hand. As I fondle it, I hear a ghostly standing ovation from hundreds of Irish ancestors who starved or fled to the land of living for what I hold here. A potato.

Garden Goddess Facial Scrub

You can grow and harvest a variety of herbs that will beautify and balance your skin in the bath, as well as release a variety of aromas that have various aromatherapy effects. Simply dry the herbs during the fall, and then place them in a cheesecloth or muslin bag, tie it off, and drop into a tub of warm water. If you don't want to grow your own, you can order all of these plus hundreds of other herbs, muslin bags, aromatherapy oils, and books on herbs. Here are some common herbs and their suggested uses for different skin types:

Dry, sensitive skin: borage, comfrey, elderflowers

Mature skin: chamomile, gingko, horsetail, lavender

Oily, blemished skin: calendula, echinacea, goldenseal, mint, sage, yarrow

- 1 medium-sized banana
- 6 strawberries, hulled
- 2 egg whites
- 2 tablespoons nonfat yogurt

Blend ingredients on high for 3 to 5 minutes. Apply to damp skin, and leave for 10 to 15 minutes.

Sandwich Mask

- ½ cup crushed avocado
- 1 large tomato
- 1 medium-size cucumber, chopped

Puree the ingredients in a blender or mixer until smooth.

Apply to skin and allow to dry. Rinse well and follow with a light toner and moisturizer.

In Pursuit of Inner Peace

Working in the garden gives me a profound feeling of inner peace. Nothing here is in a hurry. There is no rush toward accomplishment, no blowing of trumpets. Here is the great mystery of life and growth. Everything is changing, growing, aiming at something, but silently, unboastfully, taking its time.

The Healing Power of Peppermint

Peppermint is one of the easiest things to grow and now it turns out that is good for you too. Studies in Europe have shown that peppermint reduces nasal membrane inflammation, making your stuffy nose feel better. Peppermint oil also helps relieve intestinal gas and motion sickness. But according to researchers at Purdue University, there's not enough oil in commercial peppermint teas to get this effect. The good news is that it is easy to make yourself. Just harvest a big batch and allow to dry in the sun. Then store until needed. When you're feeling low, crush enough to make 2 teaspoons of crushed leaves, place in the tea strainer, and pour a cup of boiling water over the leaves. Cover and steep for 10 minutes.

Chamomile Cleanse

You don't need to go to a spa or buy any fancy equipment to enjoy a facial steam. All you need is a large pot of boiling water, a sturdy table, a handful of herbs, and a bath towel.

Bring a large pot of water to a boil. Remove from heat and add a handful each of whole sage leaves, whole peppermint leaves, and chamomile flowers. Carry the pot over to the table, along with the bath towel, and sit down in front of the pot. Drape the towel over your head and shoulders so that you and the pot are under the towel, being sure to keep your face sat least a foot away from the pot. Breathe slowly and deeply through the nose, lifting the towel to get fresh air as needed. Stay under the towel tent for 5 to 10 minutes. Moisturize your face with a good lotion. This is not recommended if you have extremely dry skin or have heart troubles, asthma, or other breathing troubles.

Steaming Tea Facial

- 1 chamomile tea bag
- 1 peppermint tea bag
- 3 cups boiling water

Place the tea bags in a large, wide-mouthed bowl or pot. Add boiling water, and allow to cool for 2 minutes. Place a clean towel over your head and the bowl (keep your face at least eight inches away from the surface of the water), and steam for 10 minutes.

Massage Is Medicinal: Mango Feel-Better Butter Bars

Dr. Andy Weil and many other wise physicians and holistic medical experts all agree that lymphatic massage is very helpful for overcoming depression and anxiety and improves health in myriad additional ways. New research shows that the lymphatic system is mainly responsible for reabsorbing cerebrospinal fluid. If you want to feel better mentally and physically, you need to learn ways to improve lymph flow through your body and brain to improve detoxification. I take this as our cue for more massage, pronto, and ways to make this healthful practice even more enjoyable and good for the skin. This simple recipe for DIY massage bars will do just that.

Gather together:

- 3 ounces shea butter
- 3 ounces beeswax
- 1 teaspoon sandalwood essential oil
- ¼ cup mango essential oil
- 1 teaspoon sandalwood essential
- Double boiler
- Soap bar molds (available at all craft stores)

Slowly heat the beeswax and shea butter in a double boiler over low heat until just melted. Remove from heat. Add essential oils in when mixture has cooled slightly and stir. Pour into soap molds and cool until hardened, approximately 2 hours. Place in freezer for a few minutes before popping bars out of molds. To use, rub massage bar onto the skin—the warmth of the skin immediately melts the bar. I store some in small travel-size tins so I have it at all times.

CHAPTER FOUR

Winter

There are two seasonal diversions that can ease the bite of any winter. One is the January thaw, the other is the seed catalogs.

—Hal Borland

JOURNALING YOUR GARDEN

You don't have to limit yourself to just the facts in your gardening journal—it can also be a place to muse, collect quotes, and keep in touch with nature's wisdom. The key is to recognize that it can be a visual record as well as a written one—dry and paste the first sweet pea your son grew, the photos of your orchid cactus in bloom; a smattering of fall leaves on the day you found out you were pregnant surrounding the poem your husband wrote on the occasion; sketch the color of the sky on a memorable winter day. Workshop leader Barry Hopkins, who calls these Earthbound Journals, suggests that you start with a blank, hardcover artist sketchbook, at least 7 ½ x 8 ½ to allow room to paste things in, an X-Acto knife for cutting, watercolors for borders, Cray-pas for flowers, etc., aerosol glue for pasting, and fixative to keep pencils and Cray-pas from smudging.

It's important that you make your own cover for the garden journal—you can use old bits of a special shirt, for example. If you have an electric drill, you can drill through the book to create a ribbon or rawhide fastener. The point is to follow your own creativity where it leads you and to imbue the book with the memories of the garden.

> To see a hillside white with dogwood bloom is to know a particular ecstasy of beauty, but to walk the gray winter woods and find the buds which will resurrect that beauty in another May is to partake of continuity.
>
> —Hal Borland

'TIS THE SEASON TO PLAN YOUR GARDEN

Winter can be hard on gardening fanatics, forced indoors to attend only to the houseplants. So I always cheer myself up by collecting all the bulb and seed catalogs that come throughout the year and saving them for a dreary January weekend. I sit down at the kitchen table with them all spread out in front of me. First I pore over the beautiful color pictures and the accompanying descriptions, fantasizing about the incredible garden I could have if money, time, and weather conditions were no object. Shirley tulips, "ivory white with purple picotee edge," a one-of-a-kind Batik Iris that has "dramatic white spatters and streaks against a royal purple ground," alboplenum, "doubly rare for being both multi-petaled and white."

After I have completely satisfied my eyes, I get real. I make a map of my vegetable and flower gardens, check out what seeds I have left from last year, and plot out what I want to plant. Then I go back over the catalogs again with a more selective eye and choose what I really need. Often this process goes over many days and both parts give me great pleasure: the indulging of my wildest gardening fantasies, and the anticipation of color, beauty, and form in my actual garden.

Winter is the perfect time to fantasize about future gardens. The moon garden is one that has only white flowers. It's particularly striking at the moment of summer twilight when all colors except white fade and anything white takes on a luminescence that is breathtaking. That makes it a wonderful spot for evening entertaining and for those of us who work so late we only ever see our gardens in moonlight. I once went to the house of a man who was completely colorblind—any color except white or black was gray to him. He had a huge estate landscaped in beautiful, all-white beds. What stood out, of course, were the differences in textures and shapes: the airy froth of baby's breath combined with the dense snowballs of hydrangeas and the feathery spikes of cleomes.

For a dramatic garden design, you don't have to necessarily choose all white. It could be all pink or all blue or all yellow. And color doesn't have to be the only theme. A friend recently told me of a garden she'd just seen in Colorado that was only native grasses of all shapes, colors, and textures. Perhaps you are attracted to the flowers in an English cottage garden or the stylized greenery of a formal Italian garden. The point is that winter offers a great chance to imagine just what kind of outer landscape we want to create. That in itself is quite a pleasure.

> The snowdrop is the prophet of the flowers: it lives and dies upon its bed of snows; and like a thought of spring it comes and goes.
>
> —George Meredith

LAVENDER TINCTURE

This cure-all should be kept on hand at all times for soothing the skin, the stomach, and anything in need of comfort. I have even seen it used to stanch bleeding in small cuts. You need:

- **Dried lavender**
- **Clear quart jar with lid**
- **Cheesecloth**
- **Dark glass jar for storage**
- **2 cups distilled water**
- **1 cup clear alcohol such as vodka**

Fill your clear quart jar to the halfway point with the dried lavender. Pour in the alcohol also to the halfway point. Add in the water and seal with the lid securely and shake for a few minutes until it seems well mixed. Store in a dark cupboard for one month, shaking once a day. After 30 days, strain with cheesecloth into the dark glass storage jar and screw the lid on tightly. The lavender leavings will make lovely compost and the liquid tincture will soon prove itself indispensable in your household.

WINTER WONDERS

Sometimes I think the garden is even more beautiful in its winter garb then in its gala dress of summer. I know I have thought so more than once when every leaf and branch was clothed with a pure garment of snow, so light as not to hide the grace of form. But nothing, it seems to me, could ever transcend the exquisite beauty of the vegetation when, on one occasion, a sharp frost followed a very wet fog. The mist driven by the wind had imparted a coating of fresh moisture, evenly distributed, over and under every leaf and twig, inside the trees and shrubs as well as outside. The light coating then froze and left every innermost twig resplendent with delicate white crystals. It was quite different from the ordinary frost or a fall of snow, beautiful as the effects of these frequently are. But the glory of the scene reached its climax when the sun came out and the thicket scintillated from the center as well as its external surface.

The dazzling splendor, however, could not last, and the glistening and enchanted spectacle gradually melted away before the greater and more glorious life-giving presence of "God's lidless eye." This gorgeous scene, however, has always dwelt in my memory and figures as the most glowing aspect a garden can assume at any season of the year.

> I prefer winter and fall, when you feel the home structure in the landscape—the loneliness of it—the dead feeling of winter. Something waits beneath it—the whole story doesn't show.
>
> **—Andrew Wyeth**
>
> The word "miracle" aptly describes a seed.
>
> **—Jack Kramer**

SAVORING THE GARDEN

In the winter, some of my most powerful garden pleasures come from memory:

- That moment when you stop trying to keep your nails clean, take off your gloves, and dig wholeheartedly and carelessly into the dirt.
- Admiring that perfect rosebud with tiny kisses and not picking it.
- Biting into sun-warmed, perfectly ripe strawberries.
- Eating anything you've grown in your garden.
- Having a ladybug land on your arm.
- Showering outside after working in the yard on a hot summer day.
- The ruby and green flash of a hovering hummingbird.
- Pressing your nose into a bed of moss.
- Planting flowers in someone else's garden that they won't find out about until next spring.
- The smell of honeysuckle drifting in the kitchen window.

LAVENDER LOVE MASSAGE BARS

Massage bars should look, smell, and feel luxurious. Cocoa butter is beloved for its delicious chocolate scent. I also recommend shea butter or mango butter as other options, for they are also sumptuous.

- 3 ounces cocoa butter
- 3 ounces beeswax
- 3 ounces almond oil
- 1 teaspoon of lavender essential oil
- soap bar molds (available at all craft stores)

Slowly heat the beeswax, almond oil, and cocoa butter in a double boiler over low heat until just melted. Remove from heat. Add essential oil when mixture has cooled slightly. Pour into soap molds and cool until hardened, approximately 2 hours. Place in freezer for a few minutes before popping bars out of molds. To use, rub massage bar onto the skin—the warmth of the skin immediately melts the bar. Package your handmade massage oil in a pretty bottle and give it as a thoughtful gift.

BEYOND RULES

I believe in just taking my cup of coffee and clippers out to the garden in the morning and snipping here and there. Do what you want. That way, there's never this awful feeling that the fourteenth of February is Valentine's Day and your roses must be fed promptly on Valentine's Day. People's lives are regimented enough without all that.

SEED SAVERS EXCHANGE

For more than two decades, members of the nonprofit, grassroots organization Seed Savers Exchange (SSE) have been searching the countryside for "heirloom" varieties of vegetables and fruits. Kent and Diane Whealy founded SSE in 1975, after Diane's grandfather entrusted them with the garden seeds that his parents had brought from Bavaria. The Whealys began searching for other gardeners who were also keeping heirloom varieties and soon discovered a vast, little-known genetic treasure.

Today SSE's thousands of members are working together to collect, maintain, and distribute thousands of heirloom vegetables and fruits. Last year one thousand of SSE's members used Seed Savers Yearbook, one of three annual publications, to distribute the seeds of eleven thousand rare food crops to other interested gardeners. Each year, SSE's members offer twice as many varieties as are available from the entire mail-order garden-seed industry in the US and Canada. Since it was founded in 1975, SSE's members have distributed an estimated 750,000 samples of heirloom seeds that are not available in catalogs and are often on the verge of extinction. If you would like to donate or receive heirloom seeds (or both), consider joining. Check out www.seedsavers.org

What to Do in Winter

Winter is the time for doing all those garden tasks we were too busy to tackle during the rest of the year. As you've transplanted things, chances are you've accumulated a goodly number of empty pots. Winter is when you should scrub those pots with bleach so you can use them again without taking the chance of infecting your new plants with old bugs. This is also the time to sterilize any dirt (200° F in oven for 3 hours) you might want to use for spring houseplant repotting.

THE HEALING POWER OF FLOWERS: FLORAL ESSENCES ENERGIES

Many of our favorite flowers have distinctive healing energies. A key difference is that flower essences minister to the emotional body, while essential oils treat the physical body.

However, vials of a multitude of these are available at grocers, pharmacies, and new age shops. Bach Flower Remedies are doubtless the most popular and are seemingly everywhere, with a recommended dosage of 3 to 4 drops taken via the bottle dropper under the tongue 2 to 4 times a day. I suggest not using more than 2 different floral waters at any given time for full effect. Flower essences are typically ingested directly via the mouth or by way of adding a few drops to a glass of water. They can also be dropped onto linens such as your pillowcase, a sachet, or into your bath. They can be applied directly to the pulse points, such as temples and wrists. These floral essences are also different from essential oils in that they do not carry the scent of the flower. It takes a single flower to make an essence, whereas essential oils rely on a significant amount of the plant. Here are some essences that are good for emotions:

- **Passion flower** connect us to our higher self
- **Lemon blossoms** clear away mental fog, add focus, and bring forth clarity
- **Hibiscus** awakens chakra points and is good for higher energy
- **Nasturtium** stops overthinking and worry
- **Grape hyacinth** releases past trauma and emotional wounds and reduces stress

> Despite March's windy reputation, winter isn't really blown away: it is washed away. It flows down all the hills, goes swirling down the valleys, and spills out to sea. Like so many of this earth's elements, winter itself is soluble in water.
>
> —Hal Borland

SPICE UP YOUR LIFE: CINNAMON LIQUEUR

This popular beverage gives peppy energy and can also be a divine after-dinner drink. These few ingredients can lead to a lifetime of enjoyment:

- **2 cloves**
- **1 teaspoon ground coriander seed**
- **1 cinnamon stick**
- **1 cup vodka**
- **1 cup simple sugar syrup**

Pour the vodka into a bowl and add in the herbs; cover and place in cupboard for two weeks. Strain and filter until the result is a clear liquid, into which you add the simple syrup and place back on the shelf for a week. Store this in a pink- or red-capped bottle; you now have liquid love. You can add this to hot chocolate, water, tea, or milk for a delightful drink to share with a partner.

FLORAL ELIXIRS

You can make simple syrup, a base for any liqueur, in five short minutes by boiling a cup of sugar in a half cup of water. The method above can be used to create distinctive after-dinner drinks and digestives from angelica, anise, bergamot, hyssop, all mints, fennel, and, maybe the most special of all, violets. To your health!

THE WINTER GARDEN

The last handful of yellow leaves cling to the tips of the favorite apple tree—the one with the thirty-eight grafts that, in the summer, shades the north court. The dawn redwood sheds its bright, rusted foliage almost overnight, making a fine fluffy blanket for the azalea bed below. The garden has started its winter sleep. But not the birds!

The first notes I hear these frosty mornings as I let out the dogs are, *Chit, chit!* from the big hachiya persimmon on the hill. Fluttering about the bare branches, white tail spots flashing, is a pair of Audubon's warblers, down from the snowy mountains and probably on their way to even warmer climates to the south. They have stayed here almost three weeks.

This has been a good year for toy and berries, and all December I have enjoyed of bright sprays viewed through the sink window. Today the cedar wax wings arrived, and that signaled the end of the berries. Fair enough. I have enjoyed them; now it's the birds' turn. The news spread fast. There was only a quintet of black swings swinging upside down to (how do they swallow up bill?), but several Robins, who have ignored the berries up to today, arrived to help out.

Lots happening in the winter garden!

AIR CLEANERS YOU CAN GROW

Plants provide a haven, even in a small studio apartment. They improve the air we breathe and lend their seasonal beauty. This is a great idea for home and work. Not only are they pretty to look at, they are improving the air you breathe. These air-purifying plants look great, produce oxygen, and can even absorb contaminants like formaldehyde and benzene, which are commonly off-gassed from furniture and mattresses.

Here are the plants to purify the air in your home 24/7: bamboo, weeping figs, rubber tree, spider plant, peace lily, snake plants. Houseplants need their leaves dusted, so you can do this with a banana peel. The dust clings to the peel and the leaves are nourished by the peel. Go bananas!

> Who loves a garden loves a greenhouse too.
>
> —William Cowper

TAKE THE GARDEN INSIDE

In the winter, when the garden is dry and bare, nothing gives me more pleasure than a visit to the local garden shop, where it always feels like sweet, balmy summer. I wander through the rows of brightly colored flowers and richly hued, shiny leaves, and the aromas of blossoms and sweet rich earth make me forget, for a time, the gloom and doom outside. The plants and flowers are completely oblivious to the weather outside, and their verdant outbursts of energy restore my own. I take an inordinate amount of time picking out some ridiculously expensive and riotously colored plant that just screams warm weather, which I take home and place on my windowsill or bedside table in a beautiful basket or brightly colored cachepot. I have kind of a brown thumb, so my plants never last long, but I almost prefer that; it gives me a chance to go to the garden shop again that much sooner.

TOPIARY TRICKS

If you are attracted to the topiaries you see at botanical gardens, you might want to try growing one of your own. First you need a frame. Some home and garden stores are now carrying them, but you can also get them from hardware stores. Then you pick a plant to cover it with. You must think about where the topiary will be—sun or shade? Is it small enough to be brought inside in winter, or must the plant be winter-hardy? Then you must think of the plant itself—does it shear nicely (to keep the shape, you must give it a haircut regularly)? Is the leaf size in proportion to the frame, and will the texture be right for your desired effect?

Good topiary plants include ivy, star jasmine, purple bell vine, Japanese boxwood, pyracantha, rosemary, and compact myrtle.

> Everything in nature invites us constantly to be what we are.
>
> **—Gretel Ehrlich**
>
> Nature: The Unseen Intelligence which loved us into being and is disposing of us by the same token.
>
> **—Elbert Hubbard**

THE PLEASURE OF PERIWINKLE

Growing older has shown me the value of ground covers: hale survivors, they are. Ground covers do just what their name promises, at varying rates of speed. My favorite is periwinkle (or *Vinca minor*)—deep evergreen foliage whose vines hug the ground and will grow up a hill or along a wall in the poorest of soil. I placed one tiny plant alongside the chimney of my house, a place that had defied other plants. It thrives there still and has spread over the years to cover an entire hill. A few years ago, I undertook a scholarly research project about *Gawain and the Green Knight*, the epic poem in Middle English. To my great surprise and delight, I discovered that mysterious women had embroidered periwinkle onto Gawain's cape before his heroic journey to confront the monstrous Green Knight. As I dug deeper in the arcana section of my library, I discovered that periwinkle had been made into wreaths and placed on the heads of young men going to battle in medieval England. What a rich history my favorite humble ground cover comes from!

> In his garden every man may be his own artist without apology or explanation. Here is one spot where each may experience "the romance of possibility."
>
> —Louise Beebe Wilder

WITH FAMILY AND FRIENDS

> How can those who do not garden, who have no lot in the great fraternity of those who watch the changing years as it affects the earth and its growth, how can they keep warm their hearts in winter?
>
> —Mrs. Francis King

A Memory Garden

It all started when my father died and friends gave me a white rhododendron as a sympathy gift. I noticed that every year when it bloomed, memories of my father would come flooding back. Then my husband's mother died, and friends sent a crab apple tree. When that burst into bloom, we would think of her as well. We decided to turn that whole section of our yard into a memory garden: the early blooming azalea my daughter, who lives in California, sent me for Mother's Day; the scented geraniums my old friend Kay once gave me a slip of; the weeping cherry we planted in honor of my husband's father; the clematis that was my husband's holiday gift from his sister. Now, as the seasons turn and the plants bloom in turn, our thoughts go out to the person the plant symbolizes, and we draw him or her close once again. What should you grow in your memory garden?

> A garden is a place to feel the beauty of solitude.
>
> —Bob Barnes

Plant a Birthday Tree

You don't have to wait till someone dies or moves away to have a plant in their honor. My husband and I planted a hydrangea that was on the altar at our wedding. It moves with us from house to house as a symbol of our marriage. And many people have planted birth trees for their children. You can involve your child in helping take care of the tree and track its growth by tying a bit of yarn to the outermost tip of a branch each fall and seeing where the yarn ends up after the summer.

Stealing Beauty

Long ago, ladies considered houseplants very precious. When they secured a new variety, they would guard it jealously. My mother, who was sometimes a bit naughty, would carry a folded bread wrapper in her purse (plastic bags being unknown at the time), just in case she could talk someone into giving her a "slip" (as cuttings were called in those days). Once, she could not resist, when her hostess was out of the room preparing refreshments, snipping off a tiny bit of a cherished plant and slipping it into her purse. She carefully tended the cutting and it grew. Every time her friend came over I had to run out and hide it. One day she came over unexpectedly, and I remember what a dreadful time my mother had trying to explain.

> Everybody needs beauty as well as bread, places to play in and pray in, where Nature may heal and cheer and give strength to body and soul alike.
>
> —John Muir

Find Your Gardening Friends, Join a Gardening Club

For as long as I can remember, my mother belonged to a garden club. Once a month, throughout the year, she would go off somewhere, no matter where we lived. It was all very mysterious to me; what did those ladies do together? About once a year, it would be her turn to host the club, and she would work even more diligently in her flower beds, making them perfect. I remember tea and bearded iris in bloom.

Throughout the country, garden clubs continue to be popular, especially among the retired set. If you are interested in joining one, just ask around at your local nursery. If time during weekdays is an issue for you, consider the National Home Gardening Club. Dues are only one dollar per month and membership includes a number of unique benefits, such as product-testing privileges (companies send their latest products such as mowers, rakes, and hoses, and members try them out, issue a report, and get to keep them), your garden photos and garden tips published in their how-to magazine, a directory of public gardens, free plants, and member-only product offers. If you are interested in joining, check out wwwgardenclub.org.

> He who plants a garden plants happiness.
>
> —Chinese proverb

FAITHFUL GROUND COVER

My great aunt Ida had an intriguing plant that grew everywhere on her place in attractive clumps. It never bloomed, but I noticed that it looked nice beside other plants, with its low mass of green and white variegated leaves. It seemed to make the other plants it grew near look even better. Aunt Ida, a hardy ninety years old at that time, claimed she had come to depend on it to cover unattractive well covers, eave spouts, and the like. Eventually, I came away from her house with a small clump that I put in problem areas where nothing else seemed to want to grow. I especially liked that Aunt Ida's plant couldn't be found at the nurseries I dragged my mother to every weekend. But best of all, I loved the name of Aunt Ida's faithful ground cover, which conjured up images of far-off places. She called it "Snow on the Mountain."

> How doth the little busy bee Improve each shinning hour, and gather honey all the day from every opening flower?
>
> —Isaac Watts

ORNAMENTAL PLEASURES

Both these ornaments are so easy to make, they are perfect for young kids (if you help with a glue gun). Make lots—save some for your trees and give the rest away as presents to teachers, the mailman, Grandma, etc.

- **Small pinecones**
- **Seven-inch lengths of very narrow ribbon**
- **dried rosebuds**
- **glue gun**

Note: The size of the ribbon and the roses should be proportionate to the size of the cones.

Place pinecones in a paper bag. Put into the microwave and heat for 8 to 10 minutes. (This is to kill any bugs.) If you want the cones to open and this hasn't opened them, keep heating the same way at 3-minute intervals until they open.

Take the ribbon, fold it in half, and hot-glue the ends to the cone. Take a bud or two and hot-glue them on top of the ribbon ends to hide them. Repeat until all cones are gone.

Citrus Ornaments

- **3 to 4 lemons, oranges, and/or limes**
- **gold cord**
- **various small dried flowers and leaves**
- **berries, narrow ribbon, and other decorative items**
- **glue gun**

Cut the fruit into ¼-inch slices. Place four layers of paper towels on a microwave-safe plate and arrange the citrus slices on the paper towels. Bake at medium for 2 minutes at a time, allowing the citrus slices to cool between baking. After three cycles, you should have dried fruit. (If they don't all fit in one layer, do it in batches.) Cut the gold cord into six-inch lengths. One piece for each slice. Fold cord in half and glue the ends together to the back of a citrus slice. Pick out various dried flowers, leaves, and bits of ribbon and other trim, and glue them to the front of the slice.

FIRE STARTERS

A great, easy, and inexpensive gift for older kids to make for the holidays is Fire Starter Pinecones. Simply gather a quantity of dried pinecones. Heat a block of paraffin in the top of a double boiler. As it melts, add one red crayon and a few drops of cinnamon or pine essential oil. When the paraffin is completely melted and stirred, grasp a pinecone with a pair of old tongs, and dip it completely in the wax. Set on a piece of waxed paper to cool and harden. Place hardened cones in a basket, add a ribbon, and Viola!

> All my hurts
> My garden spade can heal.
>
> **—Ralph Waldo Emerson**

INTO THE KITCHEN

> Property is for the comfort of life, not for the accumulation of wealth. A sage, having been asked who is lucky and who is not, replied:
> "He is lucky who has eaten and sowed, but he is unlucky who has died and not enjoyed."
>
> **—Sa'di**

Spiced Red Wine with Brandy and Citrus

This is a bit different from mulled wine because it is served at room temperature. You must start at least three weeks in advance.

- 1 orange, peeled and sliced (keep the rind)
- ½ lemon, sliced
- 1 vanilla bean
- 6 whole cloves
- 1 750-ml bottle dry red wine
- ½ cup framboise eau-de-vie (clear raspberry brandy) or other brandy
- 6 tablespoons sugar

Combine sliced orange and lemon, orange rind, vanilla bean, and cloves in large glass jar. Pour wine over. Cover and place in cool, dark area for two weeks.

Strain wine through several layers of cheesecloth into 4-cup measuring cup. Discard solids. Add framboise and sugar to wine; stir until sugar dissolves. Pour mixture into wine bottle or decorative bottle. Cork and place in cool dark area for at least 1 week. Can be made 6 weeks ahead. Store in cool dark area. Makes about one 750-ml bottle.

Lemon Geranium Sponge Cake

This old-fashioned treat can be made any time of the year.

- ½ cup honey
- 3 tablespoons flour
- ¼ cup fresh lemon juice
- 1 teaspoon grated lemon peel
- 2 eggs, separated
- 1 cup milk
- 5 drops geranium oil
- rose geranium leaves, optional

Preheat oven to 325° F. Beat together honey, flour, lemon juice, and peel. Add yolks, milk, and geranium oil and mix again. In a separate bowl, beat egg whites until stiff, and fold into the lemon mixture. Pour into a buttered eight-inch-square baking pan and place that in a pan of hot water. If available, lay fresh rose geranium leaves on top of the pudding. Bake for 45 to 50 minutes or until cake is set and knife comes out clean. Serve warm. Serves six.

> The best thing to do with water is to use a lot of it.
>
> —Philip Johnson on designing fountains

Sprout Your Own

Back in my college days, I used to be in charge of making the sprouts and yogurt for the week. To this day, twenty years later, I can't bring myself to buy sprouts from the store. It's just too easy (and satisfying) to do on your own.

Raw sprouts are a wonderful source of vitamins. Any beans—soy, fava, lima, pinto, garbanzo—can be sprouted, as can alfalfa, sunflower, peas, lentils, and many other seeds. Just be sure never to try potatoes or tomatoes—the sprouts are poisonous. And don't sprout seeds that have been sold for garden planting: they're probably been treated with a fungicide. Untreated seeds are available at health food stores. Every seed takes a slightly different amount of soaking and sprouting time. For complete details for various sprouts plus recipes, see *Sprouting for All Seasons* by Bertha B. Larimore, published by Horizon and available by calling (801) 295-9451.

> One day, the gardener realizes that what she is doing is actually teaching herself to garden by performing a series a series of experiments.
>
> —Margaret Roach

Alfalfa Sprouts in a Jar

- 2 tablespoons alfalfa seeds
- 1 wide-mouth quart jar
- water
- cheesecloth
- rubber band

Place the seeds in the bottom of the jar and fill with water. Put cheesecloth over the top and secure with a rubber band. Store in a warm, dark place, like a kitchen cupboard. Two or three times a day, take the jar out, empty the water and add fresh water. They will be ready in 4 to 5 days and will keep up to a week in the refrigerator. Makes 1 quart.

Snug Snacks: Spiced Almonds

For the nut lovers on your shopping list, make your own spiced nuts. Package in a beautiful tin with a pretty bow.

- 2 tablespoons butter
- 1 teaspoon cinnamon
- 1 teaspoon ground cumin
- 1 teaspoon ground coriander
- 2 ½ cups raw almonds
- ¼ teaspoon (or more, depending on taste) cayenne pepper
- 2 tablespoons sugar
- 1 teaspoon salt

Preheat oven to 300° F. In a large skillet, melt the butter and add cinnamon, cumin, coriander, and cayenne. Cook, stirring constantly, about 30 seconds, until very fragrant. Add the nuts, stir to coat. Then add sugar and salt and stir again. Transfer to baking sheet and bake, stirring occasionally, until nuts are roasted, about 20 minutes. Will store up to one month if in a tightly sealed container.

Winter-Fresh Herbs

One benefit of an herb patch in your garden is that you can just pick what you need for that night's dinner: no worrying about fresh parsley or basil rotting in the bottom drawer of the fridge. But even inveterate gardeners end up having to buy herbs outside of the growing season and keeping them fresh can be a real struggle. If you follow a few simple tips, however, you can greatly expand their life. The trick is to treat them as you would cut flowers.

First, untie and immerse in cool water. Don't run under the faucet, that can damage tender leaves. Pick through and discard any rotting stems or leaves. Shake herbs dry gently; never use a salad spinner—it's too rough. Place the bunch, stems down, in a vase or canning jar that allows the leaves to stay above the rim. With basil, just store on your countertop; it will keep up to a month and may even sprout roots. With all other fresh herbs, loosely cover with a plastic bag and stick in the refrigerator. Change water every few days. Chervil, chives, dill, thyme, and watercress will keep up to a week like this; cilantro and tarragon, two weeks, and parsley as long as three weeks.

Herbaceous Bread

- 1 teaspoon sugar
- 4 cups warm water
- 1 tablespoon yeast
- 12 cups bread flour
- 1 tablespoon salt
- 3 tablespoons chopped fresh basil
- 2 tablespoons chopped rosemary
- 1 cup sun-dried tomatoes, drained and chopped
- ⅔ cup olive oil
- extra oil and rosemary for top

In a small bowl, combine sugar, ⅔ cup water, and yeast. Let sit in warm spot until frothy, about 10 minutes. In a large bowl, combine the flour, salt, herbs, and tomatoes. Add the oil and the yeast mixture, then gradually add the remaining warm water. As dough gets stiff, mix with your hands until it is soft but not sticky.

Turn onto a lightly-floured surface and knead for 5 minutes. Place back in bowl, cover with a towel and place in a warm spot until doubled in size, about 40 minutes.

Preheat oven to 425° F. Knead again until elastic, then cut into three equal pieces. Shape each into a round and arrange on oiled baking sheets. Brush a bit of oil on each loaf and top with a few rosemary leaves. Bake until golden brown and hollow-sounding when tapped, about 25 minutes. Makes three 7-inch loaves.

Provencal Potatoes

This hearty French dish is a perfect winter accompaniment to grilled or roasted meat.

- 1 ½ pounds potatoes, sliced
- 4 shallots, sliced
- Three garlic cloves, sliced
- Salt and pepper to taste
- 1 teaspoon chopped fresh thyme, or ¼ teaspoon dried
- ½ cup dry white wine
- ⅔ cup pitted black olives such as nicoise or kalamata

Preheat oven to 375°F. Combine all ingredients in a casserole dish and bake uncovered until potatoes are tender and liquid is absorbed, about 30 to 40 minutes. Stir occasionally and add a bit of water if necessary. Serves four.

Aromatic Trivet

This is a kitchen delight that will release a fabulous fragrance into the air every time you place a hot pan on it. It's so simple to do, you should consider making some for yourself and for your friends.

- twenty inches of sturdy fabric, such as mattress ticking
- scissors
- needle and thread
- stuffing: broken cinnamon sticks, cloves, and bay leaves
- upholstery needle
- cotton string

Cut two 20- to 25-inch pieces of fabric and place right sides together. Pin and stitch the pieces together, leaving an opening large enough for the stuffing to fit through. Trim the seams and turn right-side-out. Fill with stuffing material and then slip-stitch the opening, using the upholstery needle threaded with string. Make four separate stitches in the center of the pad, forming a square, clearing the contents away from the stitch. Finish each with a simple knot. Makes one pad.

Make Your Own Vanilla Extract

You can do it, and it is unbelievably easy. If you place it in a pretty glass bottle, it makes a lovely little gift.

- 1 vanilla bean
- 1 4-ounce bottle with top
- Scant 4 ounces vodka

Split the bean in half, put in the bottle, and pour in the vodka. Cap and let sit at least one month. (The longer, the stronger.)

Mulled Cranberry Cider

Here's a twist on an old winter favorite.

- 4 cups cider
- 4 cups cranberry juice
- 6 cloves
- 1 stick cinnamon
- 4 whole allspice
- ½ cup brown sugar

Bring all ingredients to a simmer in a large pot, stirring until sugar melts. Strain and serve. Makes 8 cups.

Summer in a Jar

In February, I love to open the cabinet to look at the jars of tomato sauce I canned the previous August. The jars look like dark red jewels and, when opened, smell exactly like sweet summer.

> I plant rosemary all over the garden, so pleasant it is now that at every few steps one may draw the kindly branchlets through one's hand and have the enjoyment of their incomparable incense.
>
> —Gertrude Jekyll

The Simplicity of Soup

It is a wintry Sunday morning. The sun is streaming through the kitchen windows onto newly wiped counters. A sack of fresh vegetables waits on the cutting board. The beans, soaked overnight, are rinsed and in a colander, ham hocks are simmering succulently on the stove, and five gleaming white bowls stand empty by the sink. I am about to make Portuguese Bean Soup, and all is right with the world.

First the carrots, cut across, form perfect orange disks which seem to glow as they fill one of my lovely white bowls. Then the onions—*whack, whack, whack*—become immaculate pearly wedges glittering in a second bowl, side by side with the carrots. The orange and pearl are now joined by a bowl filled with pale green celery slices. Raw potato cubes add to the lineup, and soon the fifth bowl overflows with roughly shredded cabbage. A mound of lacy chopped parsley rests on the countertop. The aroma of simmering ham is soon complemented by the scent of freshly squeezed lemon juice, and then by the enticing, pungent odor of minced garlic. These glorious ingredients will soon join forces to become the feast my family and I love. Surveying the colorful, aromatic, magnificent array I have created, I feel like Mother Earth, Pablo Picasso, and Johnny Appleseed rolled into one.

BOUNTEOUS BEAN SOUP

- ½ pound dried kidney beans
- 2–3 ham hocks, sautéed
- 3 carrots, sliced
- 1 onion, sliced
- 3 stalks celery, sliced
- 2 large baking potatoes, cut into ¾-inch cubes
- 3 tablespoons parsley, minced
- 1 tablespoon lemon juice
- 2 cloves garlic, minced
- salt and pepper
- 1 8-ounce can tomato sauce
- ½ head cabbage, shredded
- 2 pounds Italian sausage, sliced thinly
- ½ cup uncooked macaroni

Soak the beans in water overnight. Simmer the ham hocks in water high enough to cover them for 1 ½ hours. When tender, remove, discard bones, shred meat, and set aside. Add the drained beans to the broth and cook for 1 hour. Add the carrots, onion, celery, potatoes, parsley, lemon juice, garlic, salt, pepper, and tomato sauce, and cook until vegetables are tender. Add cabbage, sausage, and macaroni and cook until the macaroni is done. Serves six.

Almost Home-Grown

Okay, so this story isn't about my own garden, but about someone else's. About six months ago, I saw an ad for organic produce, delivered weekly to your door. I called the number and decided to sign up because the price—twenty-five dollars for enough vegetables for two people for a week—sounded like no more than I pay at the grocery store (and a lot less than those fancy natural food stores). I've been delighted. The box shows up on my doorstep every Friday afternoon, and it gives me great pleasure to eat only organic foods and to help provide employment for small farmers. Eating in season, though, has taken some getting used to—in the winter, there was a time when I thought if I had to eat another eggplant I was going to go nuts, and right now we're suffering from an overabundance of basil—and I still supplement occasionally by buying something I can't live without from the store. But it has made me eat things I would have never bought (spring garlic shoots are incredible!), and I find I'm eating more fruits and vegetables in general than ever before. Mostly I like the groundedness of it all—when it's spinach season, that's what you eat; when there are peaches, you can have them. And when the season is over, that's it till next year. Just another way of reminding me of the cycle of life.

Cozy Winter Stew

- 2 tablespoons olive oil
- ¼ cup green bell pepper
- 1 cup chopped onion
- 4 cloves chopped garlic
- 2 cups chopped fresh spinach
- 2 cups chopped cabbage

- 1 14½-ounce can tomatoes
- 1 cup frozen lima beans
- 4 ounces fully cooked sausage, such as andouille (for a spicier stew) or kielbasa, sliced
- ¼ cup chopped parsley
- 2 14 ½ ounce cans of beef, chicken, or vegetable broth

In a large pot, heat the olive oil over medium-high heat and add green pepper, onion, and garlic. Sauté until vegetables are tender, about 5 minutes. Add the remaining ingredients and simmer until cabbage is cooked, about 10 minutes. Serves four.

Perfect Poached Fruit

When the weather turns cold, I always get a hankering for poached winter fruit. Here's one of my favorite recipes.

- 2 cups sugar
- 4 cups water
- 1 lemon, cut in half
- 2 sticks cinnamon
- 4 cloves
- 6 whole allspice
- ¼ teaspoon nutmeg
- 3 apples, peeled and sliced
- 3 pears, peeled and sliced
- 1 orange, peel on and sliced crosswise into very thin slices
- 2 cups fresh cranberries
- ¼ cup dried fruit

Combine the sugar and water in a large heavy saucepan over medium-high heat and cook until sugar is dissolved. Squeeze lemon into the pot, then add the rind. Add the spices and simmer for about 5 minutes to blend flavors. Add fruit and cook only until fruit is tender, about 5 to 10 minutes. Remove lemon rind and serve warm. Serves six.

The Comfort of Cooked Cabbage

Winter is cabbage season, and there are all kinds of delicious ways to serve this whole head.

- 1 tablespoon plus ½ cup olive oil
- Six small leeks, cut in half lengthwise and well cleaned
- One small head of cabbage
- 2 cups water
- 4 tablespoons white wine vinegar
- 1 tablespoon Dijon mustard
- Salt and pepper to taste

In a large frying pan, heat the 1 tablespoon olive oil over medium heat and add the leeks. Sauté for 2 minutes. Core the cabbage and cut into six equal pieces. Add the water and 3 tablespoons vinegar. Cover and simmer for 10 minutes, then uncover and simmer for 30 minutes, until vegetables are tender and most of the liquid has cooked off. As the cabbage is cooking, in a small bowl, combine remaining 1 tablespoon of vinegar and mustard. Whisk into the pan and stir. When vegetables are done, drain off liquid and place on a serving platter. Pour dressing over and add salt and pepper to taste. Serve warm. Serves six.

> When I was most tired, particularly after a hot safari in the dry, dusty plains, I always found relaxation and refreshment in my garden. It was my shop window of loveliness, and nature changed it regularly that I might feast my hungry eyes on it. Lone female that I was, this was my special world of beauty: those were my changing styles and my fashion parade.
>
> **—Osa Johnson**
>
> A house with daffodils in it is a home lit up, whether or not the sun be shining outside. Daffodils in a green bowl—and let it snow that it will.
>
> **—A. A. Milne**

HEALING SECRETS OF THE ANCIENTS: OXYMELS

Oxymels are a very old-fashioned tonic, dating back to ancient times, which have fallen out of fashion. It remains a favorite of herbal healers and is made of two seemingly opposing ingredients—honey and vinegar. Herbs can be added to great effect, and when you see honey-menthol cough drops on the pharmacy shelf, note that origin of over two thousand years ago. Oxymels are supremely effective for respiratory issues. The recipe is simplicity itself: equal parts honey and vinegar poured over herbs in a canning jar. Store in a dark cupboard and give the sealed jar a good shake every day. After two weeks, strain out the herbs with cheesecloth and store in the fridge.

Recommended oxymel herbs: oregano, elder flower, sage, balm, mint, lemon peel, thyme, lavender, rose petals, hyssop, and fennel.

Craft Your Own Cough Drops: Candied Herbs

- 1 cup vodka
- 1 cup simple sugar syrup
- 1 cup honey
- 2 cups dried herb of choice
- 1 large sheet waxed paper

One of the by-products of making herbal honey, liqueurs, and oxymel is the candied herbs, which can also be made especially for snacks and for use in sweet cakes and cookies. To make a batch, stir the liquids together in a big pot and heat slowly, stirring every few minutes. Upon reaching boiling point, add the herbs until well mixed. Turn to a slow simmer until the liquid is very thick and sticky. Spoon the herbs out and place on wax paper to crystallize. Good herbs for this are hyssop, ginger root, lavender, lemon balm, fennel seed, mint, angelica stems, and thyme, as well as small slivers of orange, lime, and lemon. The gift of homemade candy is a marvelous way to signal a crush.

LIVING LEGACY: CHRISTMAS TREES

I have a large yard that can accommodate more trees, so every Christmas we buy a small live evergreen. We decorate it with popcorn and cranberry strands and, when the holidays are over, plant it outside, complete with decorations. The birds love it!

We decorate our live Christmas tree with tiny bouquets of dried flowers and use thin ribbon as hangers. We also bundle cinnamon sticks together with raffia and hang them from our tree, along with bundles of small pinecones and holly twigs that we wire together with garden wire.

APPLE POMANDERS

Stud apples with whole cloves, then roll them in a mixture of equal parts ground cinnamon, nutmeg, cloves, and orris root (available at herb stores and through herbal catalogs). Let dry in a warm, dry, dark place. When dry, place in a bowl to fill a room with a delightful aroma.

> If Eve had had a spade and known what to do with it, we should not have had all that sad business about the apple.
>
> —Elizabeth von Arnium

EASY SEASONAL CENTERPIECE

This beautiful old table arrangement of candles and greens couldn't be simpler to make; just be sure to use dripless candles.

- shallow waterproof bowl
- large circular plate
- florist foam
- florist tape

- small pinecones
- florist wire
- cinnamon sticks, cut to two-inch lengths
- narrow silver or gold ribbon
- 9 tall dripless candles
- small spruce and/or fir branches
- holly and/or ivy sprigs
- one dozen red roses

Select a bowl that is around two inches in diameter smaller than the plate and place it in the center of the plate. Cut the florist foam into a circle and soak it in water for 5 to 10 minutes, then secure it to the bowl with a crisscross of floral tape.

Take the pinecones and bundle them into groups of three or four with florist wire, tying the stems together. Leave about two inches of wire coming off the end. Wrap the cinnamon sticks in groups of three with the ribbon.

Take 4 candles and cut 1½ inches off the bottom. Take an uncut candle and push it into the center of the foam. Arrange the four other uncut candles around it, making a circle. Then take the four shorter candles and press them into the foam near the edge, creating a square. From this point on, make sure that you look at the arrangement from all angles as you work, so that the arrangement will be balanced.

Push the fir and/or spruce branches into the sides of the foam so that they are lying on top of the plate. Poke ivy and holly into the rest of the sides of the foam and around the candles to give body to the arrangement. Cut the stems of the roses so they are about six inches long. Push them into the foam among the candles and around the sides. Place the cinnamon sticks throughout to complete the centerpiece.

Holiday Celebration: Napkin Rings

These will go beautifully with the centerpiece.

- 6 bendable tree twigs, such as silver birch, long enough to be bent into a circle with a three-inch circumference
- silver or gold ribbon
- small dried red roses
- glue gun

Twist twigs into rings and fasten with floral wire. Make a small bow with the ribbon and tie onto each of the rings. Make sure that when the ring is flat on the table, the bow is also horizontal (if necessary, carefully hot-glue the bow). Next, hot-glue a small bunch of dried roses around the bow and over the knot, to create a splash of color. Makes six napkin rings.

> Even if something is left undone, everyone must take time to sit still and watch the leaves turn.
>
> —Elizabeth Lawrence

ROSEMARY RINGS

For a holiday party, decorate your serving platters with rosemary rings. Simply shape long branches into a ring, as if making a wreath, and tie with floral wire. Place it on plate and decorate branches with cherry tomatoes. You can also use shorter rosemary branches to make festive napkin rings; again secure with floral wire.

FABULOUSLY FESTIVE: POTPOURRI

Most potpourri have a major scent, often a secondary one and a fixative, usually orris root. Roses, lavender, and orange blossoms are all common flowers for the major scents. The secondary scent is usually provided by something lighter—scented geranium, delphinium, lemon verbena, mint, and bay are common, but dry them before they fade.

You can use flowers from your garden or those from a store-bought bouquet. Spread on a rack, such as a cake rack, and let them dry in a warm but shady spot. This may take a week or longer—until the petals feel dry but have not turned brittle. You can continue to gather flowers until you have all you need. Keep the dried flowers in a sealed container in a dark place until ready to be used. Mix the petals with the orris root and any other ingredients you want to add—bay leaves, cloves, allspice, roof. For each quart of petals use 1 tablespoon orris root. Stir gently and store and add an airtight container and a cool, dark place for about three weeks. Then place the potpourri in an attractive glass or ceramic jar that can be closed tightly. Open the jar to fill the room with fragrance; close it to preserve the potpourri. You can also package it up in a basket with ribbons or raffia for gift giving.

Christmas Potpourri

- 1 quart dried pine needles
- 1 ½ teaspoons essential oil such as pine or fir
- 1 ½ cup cinnamon sticks, broken in halves
- 1 cup chopped patchouli leaves
- 1 tablespoon each allspice, cinnamon, cloves, mace, and orris root
- Handful of dried cranberries

Combine the pine needles and oil in a large bowl, then add rest of ingredients. Place in a potpourri jar or glass bowl.

Gifty Potpourri

Here's a mixture you can make for holiday gifts for teachers, or for open houses and other get-togethers when you want to bring a little something. Be sure to package with directions.

- 1 cup whole allspice
- 1 cup star anise
- 1 cup ginger, cut into slices
- 2 cups orange peel, cut into slices
- 2 cups rose petals
- 2 cups lemon verbena leaves
- 30 drops allspice oil

Combine all ingredients except allspice oil in a large container. Stir in oil 5 drops at a time until mixture is well combined. Store in airtight container or, if you want to use as gifts, package in baggies or small jars.

To use, pour ½ cup into 2 to 3 cups of water and simmer gently on the stove to release aroma. Can be reheated until scent is gone. Makes about 10 cups.

IN A JAPANESE GARDEN

In order to comprehend the beauty of the Japanese garden, it is necessary to understand—or at least to learn to understand—the beauty of stones. Not of stones quarried by the hand of man, but of stones shaped by nature only. Until you can feel, and keenly feel, that stones have character, that stones have tones and values, the whole artistic meaning of a Japanese garden cannot be revealed to you. At the approaches to temples, by the side of roads, before holy groves, and in all parks and pleasure grounds, as well as in all cemeteries, you will notice large, irregular flat slabs of natural rock—mostly from the riverbeds and water-worn, sculptured with ideographs, but unhewn. These have been set up as votive tablets, as commemorative monuments, as tombstones, and are much more costly than the ordinary cut-stone columns and *hakas* chiseled with the figures of divinities in relief. Again, you will see before most of the shrines, and even in the grounds of the nearly all large homesteads, great irregular blocks of granite or other hard rock, worn by the action of torrents and converted into water-basins (*ch⊠zubachi*) by cutting a circular hollow in the top. Such are but common examples of the utilization of stones even in the poorest of villages; and if you have any natural artistic sentiment, you cannot fail to discover, sooner or later, how much more beautiful are these natural forms than any shapes from the hand of the stone cutter.

> Join the whole creation of animate things in a deep, heartfelt joy that you are alive, that you see the sun, that you are in this glorious earth which Nature has made so beautiful, and which is yours to enjoy.
>
> —Sir William Osler

ZEN CENTERPIECE

Truly nothing could be easier than this arrangement; it will foster serenity wherever you place it.

- **Small rocks**
- **Colander**
- **Shallow bowl**
- **3 small floating candles**
- **1 flower such as gardenia, rose, or hibiscus**

Place the rocks in a colander and rinse. Take the bowl and fill the bottom with one to two inches of rocks, depending on the depth of the container—you want to create a rock bottom. It sounds like rock and roll. Fill with water up to one inch from the top rim. Float the candles and gently place the blossom on the water and allow it to float.

FLOWERPOT CANDLES

Nothing can be easier than turning your old flowerpots into beautiful candle holders—wonderful for you as holiday gifts. This is a Christmas holiday scent, but feel free to substitute your own favorite essential oils. This recipe is for one candle but can be multiplied for more.

- **1 3-inch clay flowerpot**
- **small piece of self-hardening clay**
- **1 6-inch candle wick**
- **1 small stick at least 5 inches long**
- **1 ounce beeswax**
- **1 ounce paraffin wax**
- **15 drops cinnamon essential oil**
- **15 drops mandarin orange essential oil**

Plug the hole in the bottom of the pot with the clay and let harden. Attach one end of the wick to the stick. Lay the stick across the top of the pot with the wick hanging down in the center of the pot.

In a double boiler, melt the beeswax and add paraffin. When melted, remove from heat and let cool slightly. Add the essential oils and mix thoroughly.

Pour the wax slowly into the pot, reserving a little bit. Fill it to within ¼ inch of top. If a hollow forms around the wick as the wax cools, pour more wax into the hollow. Once hardened, remove stick by trimming the wick. Makes one candle.

HAPPY HOLIDAYS HOMEMADE WREATH

This is your basic green wreath that can cost so much to buy. This year, why not try making your own?

- **Wreath form**
- **Spooled green floral wire**
- **Evergreen boughs**
- **Garden trimming shears**
- **Wire cutters**
- **Decorations such as pine cones, holly, small ornaments, etc.**
- **Large bow**
- **Glue gun**

Tie the end of the spool of floral wire around the wreath form. Pick up a small bunch of evergreen bough stems. Cut them about three to five inches in length and place them on the inside of the form. Wrap the wire around the form, over the boughs, a couple of times. Wrap tightly so the boughs are fairly secure. Gather another bunch of boughs, trimming if necessary, and place next to the last bunch. Secure in place with wire. Repeat this, moving to the outside edge as you go. When you finish the first row, place the next bunch about two inches down from where you started and repeat the sequence again.

Make sure the stem ends and the wire of the previous row are well covered. Continue until you have covered the whole wreath form. Tie off the wire and cut the excess off close to the knot.

Now you can decorate the wreath with trim of your choosing. With the glue gun, glue pine cones, holly, ornaments, etc., to the wreath. Glue on bow. When you are done, take the floral wire and pass a couple of loops of the wire around the wreath form to create a hanger. Check to be sure it can't be seen when you hang the wreath up.

ORANGE & BAY GARLAND

In the back woods of Maine, I've seen this Christmassy-smelling garland made into a wreath by shaping a wire clothes hanger into a circle and using it instead of twine. It requires a bit of advance planning—you need to dry the oranges in a cooling oven after you've baked something else, before assembling the rest.

- **3 oranges**
- **metal skewers**
- **1 yard string**
- **8 cinnamon sticks**
- **100 fresh bay leaves**
- **1 large darning needle**

Make a series of vertical cuts into the oranges, but do not cut all the way through (imagine sectioning an orange with the peel on, but cut only ¼ of the way in). Thread a skewer through one of the slits, and come out the back side through another slit. Repeat for several slits. Rest the skewers across a baking pan so that the oranges are suspended over the pan. Place in a cooling oven and let sit until the orange skins have hardened. Let sit in a warm, dry place for 1 week or so to continue drying.

To make the garland, tie a knotted loop at one end of the string. Tie on a cinnamon stick next to the loop. Thread the darning needle onto the other end of the string, and then thread 10 bay leaves onto the string by skewering them through the middle with the needle. Tie another cinnamon stick on and thread another 10 bay leaves. Thread an orange through the center. Repeat until you've used up all the materials.

Makes a thirty-inch garland that can be tacked to a mantel.

> Gardening gives me fun and health and knowledge. It gives me laughter and color. It gives me pictures of almost incredible beauty.
>
> **—John E. Kenyon**

COAXING SPRING

When you've got the winter blahs, say around February or March, one of the easiest cures is to anticipate spring by forcing branches to bring a bit of color indoors. Any of a wide variety of bushes, shrubs, and trees will do, including forsythia, crab apple, pussy willows, quince, cherry, plum, pear, dogwood, privet, red maple, gooseberry, weeping willow, and witch hazel. Simply cut the edges of the branches on a slant with sharp scissors and plunge immediately into a vase of warm water. As the days pass, make sure there is plenty of clean, tepid water in the vase and the warmth of the house will do the rest of the work. Viola, instant spring!

> How can one help shivering with delight when one's hot fingers close around the stem of a live flower, cool from the shade, and stiff with newborn vigor?
>
> —Colette

NOURISHING BODY AND SOUL

> God has given us memories that we may have roses in December.
>
> —Anonymous
>
> When bad things happen, it's the time when you get to work in the garden and sort out the pots from the weeds.
>
> —Elizabeth Hurley

Learn the Healing Secrets of Aromatherapy

Aromatherapy, the use of scents from the essential oils of plants to alter mood and promote healing, is an ancient art currently enjoying a booming revival. While many common garden plants are used in essential oils—peppermint, basil, and lavender, to name a few—the quantities of flowers or leaves needed to produce the oil (a thousand pounds of jasmine flowers for one pound of oil, for example) means that even the most prolific gardeners would be better off buying their essential oils from catalogs or stores.

Most commonly, the oils are used in the bath (put in at the very end; the water should be no more than 100° F), in a diffuser, or placed on a handkerchief and inhaled when you need a lift. Since essential oils are very potent, they should always be diluted with a base oil, such as sweet almond or grape-seed oil before being put on your skin. And don't ingest or get it in your eyes. If you are pregnant or have a chronic illness of any kind, consult your physician before using any essential oils.

Here are some of the most common essential oils and their qualities:

- **Basil**: uplifting, clarifies thought processes
- **Bergamot**: uplifting, yet calming
- **Cedarwood**: relaxing, stress-reducing
- **Chamomile**: soothing and calming, excellent to use after an argument
- **Eucalyptus**: invigorating, cleansing
- **Fennel**: relaxing, warming, calming
- **Fir needle**: refreshing, cleansing
- **Frankincense**: calming, releasing fear
- **Geranium**: balancing mood swings, harmonizing
- **Juniper**: purifying, stimulating
- **Lavender**: calming, soothing, relaxing
- **Lemon**: uplifting, refreshing, mental alertness
- **Lemongrass**: stimulating, cleansing, tonifying
- **Lime**: invigorating, refreshing
- **Mandarin orange**: uplifting, refreshing
- **Marjoram**: very relaxing, anxiety-reducing
- **Myrrh**: strengthening, inspiring
- **Orange**: uplifting, refreshing
- **Patchouli**: inspiring, sensuous
- **Pine**: refreshing, cleansing, stimulating
- **Peppermint**: stimulating, cleansing, refreshing, invigorating
- **Rose**: emotionally soothing
- **Rosemary**: stimulating, cleansing, good for studying, invigorating
- **Sage**: cleansing, purifying
- **Sandalwood**: Stress-reducing, sensuous, soothing, helps release fear
- **Spearmint**: refreshing, stimulating
- **Ylang-ylang**: uplifting, sensuous

> He wanted a flower garden of yellow daisies because they were the only flower which resembled the face of his wife and the sun of his love.
>
> —Bessie Head

Aromatherapy for Kids

With the popularity of aromatherapy these days, many parents are wondering if it is safe for children. Essential oils in particular can be quite strong, and so there are a few guidelines:

1. Always dilute essential oils before applying to children's sensitive skin. You can use oils such as sweet almond, grape-seed, or jojoba for massage or skin care and liquid castile soap for shower products. But never put undiluted essential oils directly on a child's skin.
2. Shake well before using because the oils have a tendency to separate.
3. Keep all essential oils out of the reach of children. Ditto diffusers. Little children have been known to drink the oils in diffusers.

Juniper Bath Balm

Make the man in your life (or yourself) this extra-special treat this holiday season. It's amazingly simple—and if you have a bay tree, you can even get some of the ingredients from your own garden.

- ½ cup almond meal
- 10 drops patchouli oil
- 15 drops balsam oil
- 5 drops juniper oil
- ½ ounce shredded bay leaves
- ½ ounce juniper berries, crushed (use a mortar and pestle or a coffee grinder)
- 1 terry facecloth
- ½ yard string

Combine the almond meal and the essential oils in a glass bowl. Stir well with a wooden spoon to blend. Add the bay leaves and juniper berries and mix well. Open the facecloth and place on the counter. Pour the mixture onto the center of the cloth. Pick up the four corners and twist them closed as tightly as possible. Tie securely with string by winding it around it several times and knotting firmly.

To use, fill up a tub with water until almost full. Add the bath bag, giving it a squeeze when wet through. Rub the cloth over your body to remove rough skin. Delightful!

> A happy life must be to a great extent a quiet life, for it is only in an atmosphere of quiet that true joy can live.
>
> —**Bertrand Russell**

The Tao of Gardening

At one point in middle school, I became such an avid would-be gardener that I worked at a greenhouse during the summer and fancied becoming a landscaper. Working at the greenhouse was a real bonus, as I got my pick of plants and trees that came in right off the truck. After they were deducted from my meager paycheck, I hardly made lunch money! I also got to adopt and rescue (for free!) plants that were becoming root-bound in the pot or whose health was becoming endangered by baking all day in too-sunny displays. I loved saving their lives and felt I was genuinely contributing to the health and beauty of the planet.

After a long summer of working, swimming, and gardening at home, I was glad to get back to the fall routine of school. I loved watching the season change toward the restful cold-weather time of winter. Aside from some mulching and pruning, there was nothing for me to do but sit back and watch the changes in my family's yard. My family was somewhat stunned by my gardening industry. With my supplies from the greenhouse, I had transformed an "okay" lawn into an impressive showplace, complete with a little Japanese multilevel Zen garden with a Japanese maple, a pond that didn't hold water very well, and the *pièce de* résistance—a chipped pagoda I'd gotten at the nursery!

When the winter snows hit, most of my efforts were hidden from view as my treasured plants took a well-deserved rest. After a two-day blizzard, everything was under a white, fluffy blanket. My little Zen garden, however, still drew the eye. Finally, I understood the wisdom of Oriental gardeners. Their gardens were created to have changing beauty throughout all the seasons. I had only imitated what I had seen in the gardening books at the nursery. It was only in the dead of winter that I realized the red bark and leaves of the Japanese maple were stunningly beautiful against the blanket of snow. The pyracanthus climber I had planted was such a dark green as to be almost black with blazing orange berries, while the evergreen shrubs, growing free-form, took an entirely Eastern aspect next to the pagoda. Just looking at my little Zen garden in the snow filled me with inner peace.

MAMA NATURE'S HANGOVER CURE

Here's something to try, if necessary (hopefully not!), on New Year's Day.

- **1 tablespoon finely chopped fresh ginger root**
- **1 teaspoon grated lemon peel**
- **2 cups water**
- **¼ cup culinary rose water**
- **1 drop peppermint oil**

Combine the ginger root, lemon peel, and water in a covered pot and bring to a boil. Simmer 10 minutes. Strain out ginger and lemon peel pieces and cool the remaining liquid. Add rose water and oil of peppermint. Drink ½ cup at room temperature every 2 hours, along with plenty of water.

ROSEMARY RESTORES YOU

- Cotton bath bag
- 2 tablespoons grated fresh ginger
- 1 ounce fresh rosemary
- 20 drops rosemary oil
- 20 drops lavender oil
- 1 cup rose water

Place the fresh ginger and rosemary in a cotton bath bag, or bundle in a one-foot square piece of unused cheesecloth. Tie closed. Place the bag under the bathtub spigot and run under hot water. Add oils and rose water to the bathtub, swirling with your hand to combine. The bath beg makes an excellent scrubber and exfoliator, and the ginger and rosemary will leave skin pleasantly tingling and feeling revived.

LESSONS FROM THIS GOOD EARTH

The season of reflection comes every year in Northern California with the midwinter rainstorms. When it is dark for days on end, and God seems to ask for contemplation, what has the year in my garden taught me?

I gaze out at the tiny peach tree that taught me this year to be more present with the earth. In the spring, I pruned the tree late and, when the rains stopped early, I neglected to pay attention: it almost died from lack of water. I spent all summer bringing it back from the dead, treating the tree with tender care, noticing when it needed water, picking off the little brown balls of sap that formed when an insect burrowed into a branch.

Soon it will be time to prune again, and this year I will notice which branches need to be trimmed. One or two should be plenty. Those left will be what is needed for the following year. Pruning is a lesson in moderation—you need to follow the need of the tree. Not too much, not too little.

I began the winter planting three kinds of beets. My parents occasionally had beets with a meal when I was a child. They were times I don't remember fondly—oh, how horrible the taste was. That round red slice would sit on my plate, and I would eat everything else so that I could say I was too full and how wonderful the meal had been. But my parents were onto my plan and that beet had to be consumed.

All these years later, my wife innocently made a meal with beets one day this year that she had bought at the farmer's market. What a revelation. Sweet, tender, with a flavor that seems to be all its own. How many years of beets I had missed because I was convinced I didn't like them? What else has passed me by because my sense of self—I'm a person who always, who never—became too rigid? Now I grow beets of various colors to remind myself to stay open to life, to the ever-changing kaleidoscope of my being.

LOVELY LAVENDER LOTION

Try buying some beautiful bottles with stoppers and decorate them with dried lavender sprigs and a raffia bow for a beautiful gift. This is so easy you can make it for everyone on your holiday list.

- **8 ounces unscented body lotion**
- **30 drops lemon essential oil**
- **30 drops lavender essential oil**

Pour the lotion into a glass bowl and add the essential oils. Mix well. Using a funnel, fill container of choice, seal, and decorate. Makes 8 ounces.

PEACE OF MIND BLESSING BOWL

For help in sleeping, stir this mix of flower petals and essential oils in a bowl in your bedroom. The lavender is said to dispel melancholy, the rosemary nightmares, and the chamomile and marjoram act as a soporific.

- 2 cups lavender flowers
- 2 cups rosemary (flowers and leaves)
- 1 cup chamomile flowers
- 2 tablespoons marjoram
- 2 teaspoons aniseed
- 2 teaspoons orris root
- 5 drops bergamot oil

MINTY FRESH DIY LIP BALM

- 1 pound shredded beeswax (from craft store)
- 1 microwave-safe quart container
- 2 tablespoons dried mint
- piece of cheesecloth
- 1 quart container with spout
- 1 ounce aloe vera
- 20 drops liquid vitamin E
- 2 tablespoons witch hazel
- tiny plastic containers with lids (available at hardware stores or craft stores)

Take the beeswax and place in a microwave-safe quart container. Set the microwave on 50 percent power and heat until the wax is soft. Put the mint in the soft wax and heat for one minute. Stir the mixture, then heat again for another minute. (Note: Stir with a non-metal spoon so as not to flavor the liquid.) Repeat until the wax is completely melted. Take the cheesecloth and fold it in half. Strain the mixture through the cheesecloth into the quart container with spout. Discard cheesecloth. Stir in the remaining ingredients and pour into containers. Fills several containers, depending on size.

> The roses under my window make no reference to former roses or better ones; they are what they are; they exist with God today. There is no time to them. There is simply the rose; it is perfect in every moment of its existence.
>
> —Ralph Waldo Emerson

VALENTINE'S DAY TREATS

Light My Fire DIY Massage Candles

Making massage candles is very similar to making any other type of potted candle. I recommend using soy wax as it is so gentle on the skin. Soy wax is also nice and soft, so it melts easily and stays together in a puddle after melting and can be reused for us thrifty crafters. It won't irritate your skin unless you have a soy allergy—if you do, you can use beeswax instead, which is so widely used. (For example, it is in nearly every single Burt's Bees product.) It is the addition of the additional oils that prevents the wax from hardening again and enables your skin to absorb it. Essential oils or cosmetic-grade fragrance oils are also added to create a soothing atmosphere. All soap-making fragrances that are also soy-candle-safe are perfect choices for scenting your massage candles. Try the basic directions below to make your first candle. For every three ounces of wax, you'll add one ounce of liquid oil, and one quarter-ounce of fragrance. I suggest making two candles in four-ounce metal tins while you master this craft.

You will need these elements:

- 2 ounces sweet almond oil or vitamin E oil
- 6 ounces high quality soy wax
- Half an ounce essential oil
- 2 4-ounce metal tins
- 2 6-inch candle wicks

Directions

1. Melt the soy wax and oil in a double boiler over simmering water.
2. Add the essential oils and stir gently to avoid bubbling or spilling.
3. Once the wax has cooled somewhat but is still melted enough to pour, place the wicks in your containers and pour the wax.
4. Allow several hours for the candles to set and harden.
5. Trim the wicks to one-quarter of an inch above the top of the candle, and they're ready to use.

SENSUAL SCENTS FOR MASSAGE CANDLES

Traditionally, these oils are considered to have aphrodisiac properties and simply smell wonderful on your skin and in your home. Just burning the candles will be magical!

- Amber
- Cedarwood
- Cinnamon
- Clary sage
- Jasmine
- Neroli`
- Patchouli
- Rose
- Sandalwood
- Vanilla
- Vetiver
- Ylang-ylang

Touch of Love Massage Oil

- ½ teaspoon of your favorite essential oil
- 4 ounces sweet almond oil

Blend well in a bowl and then pour into a small decorative glass bottle with a top. Add a beautiful ribbon, make a card, and present to the valentine of your choice. He or she will get the idea. Be sure to shake oil well before using.

Sweet Love Bath

- 1 cup dried lavender
- 1 cup dried rosemary
- 1 cup rose petals
- ¼ cup dried lovage
- ¼ cup dried lemon verbena
- ¼ cup each dried thyme, mint, sage, and orris root
- muslin

Mix all dried herbs together and store in a covered container. When you want to take a bath, place ¼ cup of herbal mix in the center of an eight-inch square of muslin and tie tightly with a piece of string. Boil this ball in 1 quart of water for 10 minutes. Draw a warm bath, pour in the herbal water, add you and your sweetheart, and use the ball to scrub one another's bodies. Makes sixteen bath balls.

Tub Full of Love Bath Oil

Here's an aromatherapy bath to inspire sensuality and enhance vitality. Run a warm bath and when tub is nearly full, light some candles, turn off the lights, and add 15 drops cardamom oil, 10 drops ylang-ylang oil, and 10 drops patchouli oil. Relax into the water and surrender to the sensations.

SERENITY SOAK COLD REMEDY

- 2 tablespoons dried eucalyptus
- 4 tablespoons dried rosemary
- 4 tablespoons dried lavender buds
- 2 tablespoons dried rosebuds

Steep the above ingredients in boiling water for 30 minutes. Strain and add the remaining liquid to the warm (not hot) bath.

BODY HEALING BATH SALTS

Since the time of the ancients in the Mediterranean and Mesopotamia, salts of the sea combined with soothing oils have been used to purify the body by way of gentle ritualized rubs. From Bathsheba to Cleopatra, these natural salts have been used to smooth the skin and enhance circulation, which is vital to overall body health since skin is the single largest organ in the human body. Dead Sea salts have long been a popular export and are readily available at most health food shops and spas. You can make your own salts, however, and not only control the quality and customize the scent, but save money, too. The definitive benefit that is far and above the cost savings is that you can imbue your concoction with your intention, which is absolutely imperative when you are self-healing.

GARDEN OF EDEN BATH SALTS

This simple recipe recalls the scents and primal memories of that Edenic paradise.

- **3 cups Epsom salts**
- **½ cup sweet almond oil**
- **1 tablespoon glycerin**
- **4 drops ylang-ylang essential oil**
- **2 drops jasmine essential oil**

Mix well and store in a colored and securely capped glass bottle. Prepare for the ritual rub by lighting citrus- and rose-scented candles. Step out of your clothes and hold the salts in the palms of your hands before adding them to the bath.

COLORFUL SHRUBS FOR WINTER BEAUTY

- **Wintersweet**: actually flowers in the winter; prized for its sweet fragrance
- **Westonbirt dogwood**: has rich red stems that look beautiful against snow
- **Hazel**: has corkscrew branches that make a wonderful silhouette
- ***Cornus stolonifer***: has bright yellow branches
- **Sea buckthorn**: has lots of bright orange berries that last through the winter

HONEY-SAGE TEA

This may not cure your cold or flu, but it sure will make you feel better:

- 2 tablespoons honey
- Juice of 1 lemon
- 1 ounce fresh sage leaves, torn
- Boiling water

Place honey, lemon, and sage in a mug. Pour the water over and stir to dissolve honey. Cover and let sit for at least 5 minutes. Makes 1 mug of tea.

THE DAYDREAM GARDEN

I've always been a city dweller and an urbanite at heart, but I've had my dream country garden planed out in my head since I was a very little girl, down to the last stepping stone. It goes through different phases; sometimes it's a very structured and proper English Garden, complete with boxed hedges and sweet little meandering pebbled footpaths; other times I envision an austere yet serene Japanese garden, all twisted bonsai and reflecting pools filled with ponderous carp. There are days when my garden is sunny and filled with flowers of all hues, and days when a gentle rain mists the knowing pines, ferns, and grasses. Changing my daydream garden is almost as fun as reflecting upon it: a year's worth of sunny annuals can be plucked up at a moment's notice and replaced by an elaborately terraced and exotic herb garden, or row upon row of proud sunflowers. Best of all, it never needs watering, and the only pests are fat, lazy bumblebees. Someday I hope to have a real garden of my own, but I know that will never really rival the one in my head!

WHAT I GET FROM A GARDEN

Visible gratitude.

Small surprises.

Metaphors.

Antidotes for too much thought.

A place to do some thinking.

A place to slash and burn and feel good about it.

A dozen shades of green.

Solvable problems.

More than I put in.

Permission to be muddy.

A model of God's efficiency and extravagance.

A chance to see the whole wheel turn.

The feast of color.

Encounters with interesting creatures.

Patience.

A place to "practice resurrection."

Zucchini for the whole neighborhood.

A place to practice strategy on small predators.

The chance to start over.

INDEX

G

H

I

J

L

M

N

O

P

R

S

T

V

W

Z